# BASICS
# *MICROWAVE*
# *SUCCESS*

*All the know-how you need to make the most of your microwave oven, plus recipes for quick and easy meals.*

# MURDOCH BOOKS
*Sydney • London • Vancouver*

# UNDERSTANDING YOUR MICROWAVE OVEN

*M*icrowaves (small waves) are short radio waves. They travel in straight lines at the speed of light and can be reflected and concentrated. The first public awareness of microwaves came during the Second World War with the use of radar. Today, microwaves are widely used for long distance communications and many varied commercial applications. Microwaves are also used to cook food quickly for both commercial and domestic use.

Always READ THE INSTRUCTIONS carefully to have a better understanding of the product.

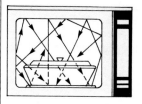

## WHAT IS A MICROWAVE OVEN?

A microwave oven has a vacuum tube, called a **magnetron**, that produces microwaves. When a microwave oven is plugged into a normal power outlet, power is fed to a transformer which converts low voltage line power to the high voltage required by the magnetron. The magnetron is the heart of the microwave oven. It converts electrical energy to microwave energy and then this energy is directed into the oven cavity along a metal guide path (or chute).

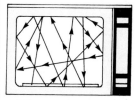

Microwaves are reflected off metal, so the walls of the oven are made of metal to improve the distribution of the waves. The oven door is also designed with a metal mesh covering to reflect the waves and keep the energy within the cavity.

The microwave oven is designed by engineers and produced by well known manufacturing companies for worldwide distribution, and therefore is guaranteed to conform to acceptable standards.

Over the years many sophistications have been introduced onto the microwave market, the most popular being electronic or touch controls. Whether the oven is a manual control, electronic touch, programmable or sensor model, the initial workings of the oven remain the same. Convection and/or browner ovens contain a heating element and circulate hot air that produces similar browning, roasting and baking results to conventional cooking.

Operating the microwave oven is best described in the instructions supplied by the manufacturer.

## HOW DOES THE MICROWAVE ENERGY COOK FOOD?

Microwaves cook by penetrating the food, causing the molecules to vibrate at an incredible rate. This creates **friction** which in turn produces heat. Unlike conventional cooking, this heat is produced in the food and not in the oven cavity, so that the interior walls remain cool.

Food cooks from the outside towards the centre. The speed of cooking depends upon the food characteristics, quantity and starting temperature of the food. Microwaves cannot penetrate more than 4 cm into the food. However, the heat generated within the outer areas of food will conduct or pass through to the centre of denser or thicker items.

When microwaves come into contact with a

substance they will do three things:

- absorb
- reflect
- transmit

Only when microwaves are **absorbed** is heat produced. Microwaves are **reflected** by metal, just as a mirror reflects light. Microwaves will also **transmit** (or pass through) materials or substances that do not contain moisture or metal. Examples are paper, glass, china, ceramic and plastic utensils. If you understand these three special characteristics of microwaves, you will find it simpler to choose suitable cooking utensils.

## POWER LEVELS — HOW DO THEY WORK?

Microwave ovens differ in power output from 450–800 W. The higher the wattage the faster foods will cook. Between 600 and 700 watts there is approximately 10% variation in cooking times. To give absolutely exact cooking times is almost impossible owing to the various microwave wattages, the quantity of food you cook and the cookware you use. Variable power levels of the microwave oven provide a range of graduated settings that allow for a choice of varying speed controls, using dials or touch controls.

## WHERE TO PLACE A MICROWAVE OVEN

A microwave oven requires no specific installation. It may be placed on a workbench, a cupboard or built into existing cupboards.

Before purchasing an oven, check external dimensions and note position of the vents. All freestanding microwave ovens require air circulation completely around the unit. If the oven is to be built in, check with the manufacturer for necessary requirements of air flow.

For ease of use a microwave oven should be positioned so the user can see into the oven without bending or stretching too high.

The oven must be placed on a *level* surface, one that is strong enough to bear the weight of the oven. Exhaust outlets must be kept clear. Keep oven away from excessive steam. Read manufacturer's operating instructions carefully before use.

## ARE MICROWAVE OVENS SAFE?

The answer is yes. Much has been written on this question and yet there are concerns and some confusion which require reassurance.

All microwave ovens sold in Britain and bearing the BEAB (British Electro-technical Approvals Board) label are made to comply with British Standard 3456. To ensure that this standard is maintained, models are independently tested at the Electricity Council Appliance Testing Laboratories for both electrical safety and microwave leakage.

Confusion possibly arises from the fact that microwaves are a form of radiation. This word 'radiation' is often misused. There are two types of radiation: the safe, non-ionising type to which microwaves belong; and the ionising type which can be hazardous, like X-rays, gamma rays and ultraviolet rays. Microwaves should not be confused with atomic or nuclear radiation or radio-activity.

There is no possible way that microwaves can be present when the oven door is opened. There need only be a slight movement to the door catch, and the microwaves will stop being generated — similar to switching off a light.

There is no proven evidence anywhere in the world of any user of a microwave oven being harmed. Food cooked in a microwave oven is not harmful to eat the moment it has been removed from the oven. The microwave oven is one of the safest kitchen appliances developed this century.

## SAFETY PRECAUTIONS

□ Never operate the microwave oven without food inside. Keep a cup or glass of water in the oven when it is not being used for cooking. If children accidentally switch on the oven, the energy will be channelled into the water, preventing any damage to the magnetron.
□ Do not use the oven for storing utensils, books or papers.
□ Do not operate the oven if it is damaged.
□ The oven should not be adjusted or repaired by anyone other than a qualified technician.

## MICROWAVE OVEN CARE

Microwave ovens are easy to clean and maintain. Clean the exterior by wiping with a damp cloth and the interior with a cloth soaked in warm soapy water. Never scour or use abrasive powders or creams in your microwave as these will scratch the surface of your oven and may lead to the distortion of the patterns of the microwaves. For stubborn stains simply fill a microsafe bowl with cold water and heat the water in the microwave until boiling point. The steam produced should loosen the food particles and they can then be wiped away.

Never turn the oven on when it is empty, as this will damage the magnetron. Do not tamper with your microwave oven in any way and use only qualified microwave technicians for repairs and service.

## AVERAGE POWER LEVEL RELATIONSHIP TO CONVENTIONAL COOKING

| CONVENTIONAL HEAT | MICROWAVE HEAT | POWER % | COOKING PURPOSE |
|---|---|---|---|
| Cool | Warm | 10–20% | warm |
| Slow | Defrost | 30–35% | defrost |
| Moderately Slow | Low | 30–40% | simmer |
| Moderate | Medium | 50–60% | poach, bake |
| Moderately Hot | Medium High | 70–80% | roast, reheat |
| Hot | High | 90–100% | sauté, boil |

When using microwave recipes, check oven wattage recommended in relationship to your own microwave oven's wattage and adjust cooking time accordingly.

# COOKWARE FOR MICROWAVE OVENS

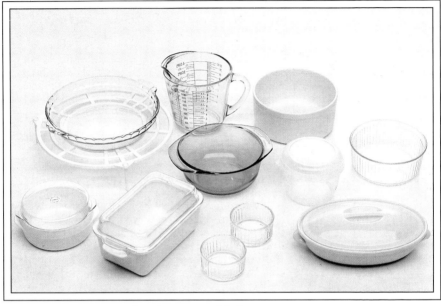

*A selection of cookware suitable for use in a microwave oven*

*W*hen selecting containers for use in the microwave oven choose for versatility, design, size, weight, cleanability and value. Suitable cookware for use in microwave ovens must be considered soon after the purchase of the oven has been made. There are many varieties of cookware that are suitable which you would probably already have in the house. Before you decide to buy new cookware it is important to understand the effects microwave energy has on various materials.

Microwave energy will:
• transmit *or pass through cookware that does not have metal or moisture in its composition.*
• reflect *off metal cookware containers or those that have a metallic composition.*

Therefore, materials that allow the microwave energy to pass through are the most suitable: glass, ceramic, plastic and paper. Refer to the Microwave Cookware chart for more detailed information.

## SUITABLE CONTAINERS

The most suitable containers to use for microwave cookery are those that are clearly marked 'Microwave Oven Safe' or those that are high heat resistant, dishwasher safe and boil-proof. Care should be taken not to use any container that could crack, warp, distort or melt. Consideration should also be given to the size and shape of containers.

As with conventional cookery the size of the container should relate to the amount of food. Too small a dish will result in spillovers, while a dish that is too large may cause overcooking of edges or an uncooked centre. Shallow dishes are best suited to foods requiring reheating only or foods requiring no stirring. Deeper containers are ideal for foods that require stirring to equalise heat distribution. Straight-sided, round or near round containers receive a more even distribution of microwave energy than containers with sharp corners, e.g. square, oblong and bar shapes. Ring moulds are ideal because the cut-out centres allow more even and quicker entry of energy into the food. Dishes that reflect microwave energy, e.g. metal pans, should not be used to cook foods in the microwave oven as the food will not cook properly around the sides and base of the pan. An exception to this rule is a Convection Microwave Oven, for which refer to manufacturer's instructions.

Bowls and wide-necked jugs are very versatile, as preparation, cooking and serving can often be done in the one container. Choose only ovenproof glass or quality plastic materials for use in the microwave oven.

Containers used in the microwave oven do not heat up from microwave energy but heat transferred from the food will cause the dishes to become hot. Depending on the type of food being cooked or the length of time the oven is operating, a pot-holder may be necessary to remove the dish and food from the oven.

Specially designed accessories are available for use in microwave ovens. It is not essential to buy all these accessories but they can provide added convenience and assist in better cooking techniques.

## PAPER

Absorbent white towels and napkins are used for covering foods to prevent spatter. They also assist in absorbing moisture during defrosting and when placed under breads, pastries etc. for reheating.

Quality greaseproof or baking paper (not waxed) gives a non-absorbent covering for cooking foods requiring moisture retention.

## CONTAINER TEST

*To test a container for suitability:*
*1  Place container (clean and dry) on glass tray in microwave oven.*
*2  Three-parts fill microsafe small bowl or cup measure with cold water and place it in or beside container.*
*3  Heat on 100% (High) power, 1–1½ minutes.*
*4  Test temperature of water, bowl or cup and the container.*
*• If water is hot, bowl is warm and outer edges of container are cold then it is SAFE for use in the microwave oven.*
*• If container is hot some microwave energy has been absorbed, making container unsafe.*
*• If any arcing or sparking occurs stop the oven, remove container and do not use.*

## PLASTIC WRAP

Plastic wrap is a valuable accessory which can be used as a cover when reheating food or for short term cooking. It forms its own seal, while still allowing steam to escape. For longer microwave cooking, special microwave plastic wrap is available. This can be used in place of a lid when cooking vegetables, etc.

Freezer bags are useful for cooking foods requiring little or no moisture, e.g. vegetables. Loosely twist the end of the bag and tuck it under. It is possible to freeze food in the bag and then place it unsealed in the microwave oven, to defrost, cook or reheat as required. Do not use twist ties to seal bags as they can melt or catch fire.

Oven bags may be used in a similar way to that employed in the conventional oven. Seal bag *loosely* with string, a rubber band or a strip cut from the top of the bag. Alternatively twist bag and tuck top of bag underneath. This will allow a small amount of steam to escape and stop pressure build-up.

## BROWNING DISHES

A variety of these dishes is available to assist in browning meat, chicken, baked vegetables and reheating pastries in the microwave oven.

There are a number of different materials used for browning dishes, all with a special coating that absorbs microwave energy. When they are placed empty in the microwave oven and preheated, the surface becomes extremely hot. When food is placed on the preheated dish the base acts as a sizzle platter searing or browning the food in a similar way to conventional hotplate frying. Care must be taken when handling the preheated dish owing to the extreme temperatures reached within the base coating.

**Browning dishes are not suitable for conventional ovens or hotplates.** Follow manufacturer's instructions for preheating times, care and cleaning.

Griddles and sizzlers perform a similar function to the browning dishes and both are also useful for scones, pikelets, pizzas, eggs, tomato and onion slices, toasted sandwiches, etc.

## COVERS

Covers are useful because they trap steam and therefore speed cooking time. Furthermore, they seal in natural moisture, preventing foods from drying out as well as preserving nutrients. Adjust covers to allow some steam to escape or too much pressure may build up within the container. Always remove any covering away from hands and face to prevent steam burns.

Suitable covers include glass or ceramic lids, ovenproof glass plates, plastic wrap and specially designed plastic microwave covers. NEVER use screw-top or similar security lids on containers. LOOSE covers, e.g. greaseproof or paper towels, are suitable to trap excess moisture and prevent spattering of some foods.

## ELEVATED AND ROASTING RACKS

Racks may be supplied with some microwave ovens; use them in accordance with the manufacturer's instructions. Multipurpose racks are used to elevate food in the oven to allow more microwave energy to reach the underside of foods. Specially designed plastic microwave racks are available for reheating more than one plate of food at a time (rearrange plates during reheating). Roasting racks manufactured in glass, ceramic and plastic are ideal for draining fats from roasts in the microwave oven.

## THERMOMETERS AND PROBES

When designed for microwave ovens, these are most suitable for ovens not equipped with an attachable or built-in temperature sensing probe. They will assist by telling you when the meat has been cooked to the degree you have programmed, i.e. rare, medium or well done.

Conventional oven meat thermometers should only be used to gauge the meat temperature AFTER it has been removed from the microwave oven — not left in during the roasting process. Follow manufacturer's directions for use.

## OTHER ACCESSORIES

**Aluminium egg rings** can be used, provided they do not come in contact with each other or the sides of the oven. **Aluminium skewers** can also be used providing they do not touch the oven wall. Bamboo skewers (pre-soaked in water) are more suitable for use when cooking kebabs or chicken.

Some special microsafe plastic cooking utensils (spoons, spatulas) are available.

## ALUMINIUM FOIL

Aluminium foil is used to shield parts of foods which might otherwise thaw unevenly, overcook or cook too quickly. Shielding stops food absorbing too much energy and slows down cooking in spots which tend to be done first. The foil must never touch the interior surfaces of the oven.

## MICROWAVE SHORTCUTS

**Peel tomatoes and peaches.** Boil a bowl of water in the microwave. Add 1-3 fruits at a time, leave for 15 seconds, then remove fruit to a bowl of cold water. The skin will peel off easily. If it doesn't, repeat the process.

**Dry herbs.** Strip leaves from stems and spread out in a single layer between absorbent paper or brown paper on a plate. Heat on 100% (High) power until herbs are dry and can be crumbled. Store in airtight containers.

## MICROWAVE SHORTCUTS

**Soften butter or cream cheese.** Unwrap, cut into pieces and place around a plate. Cook on 100% (High) power, checking for softness every 5 seconds.

**Melt or brown butter.** 60g butter takes 45-60 seconds on 100% (High) power to melt, 2-3 minutes to brown.

**Clarify butter.** Melt butter in a shallow dish on 100% (High) power until foaming. Set aside for a few minutes then pour off clear liquid. The residue can be used to flavour vegetables.

**Warm butter and sugar.** When butter and sugar are to be creamed together for a cake or biscuits, warm them first on 100% (High) power for 15-30 seconds.

**Warm plates.** Sprinkle them with water and stack them on a microwave rack or oven shelf and heat on 100% (High) power for 1 minute.

**Soften pumpkin.** Softening pumpkin makes it easier to cut. Microwave on 100% (High) power for 1½ minutes or until just warm – the amount of heating depends on the size of the pumpkin.

### Standing Time

This is an important aspect of microwave cooking. Food continues to cook by heat conduction after being removed from the oven.

Standing time allows for even heat distribution throughout the food.

It is crucial to take it into consideration when cooking meat, egg and milk dishes, bread and cakes. Allowing standing time prevents over-cooking and saves energy. The power level used in microwave cooking is a factor in determining the length of standing time.

When using low power the standing time is shorter because of the lower concentration of heat in the food. The effect of standing time is maximised by wrapping or covering the food with aluminium foil. The food will remain hot while other items are being prepared in the microwave oven.

*Tight foil cover is used with moist foods or less tender meats which need steam to cook or tenderise. Keep meats in baking dish and cover with aluminium foil. Wrap vegetables completely in foil. If casserole has a lid, place foil between it and the food to hold in heat.*

*Loose wrapping holds heat in tender meats during standing and holding time. The foil should completely enclose roast, but be loose enough to allow air to circulate.*

## MICROWAVE COOKWARE

| MATERIALS | COMMENTS | SUITABILITY |
|---|---|---|
| Glass | Sturdy glass without lead content; decorative plates or platters. | Short-term or low-power cooking; reheating |
| Ovenproof Glass | Clear containers ideal for checking process. Freezer to table or cook and serve versatility. | All forms of oven cookery |
| Pottery or Earthenware | Should be non-porous, well-glazed, no metallic content, heatproof to 180–200°C. Can become very hot during cooking. | Low-power cooking |
| China | Applicable new style china carries microwave and dishwasher safe markings. Do not use if china has metallic pattern. Do not use fine bone china. | Reheating |
| Paper | Plastic-coated paper containers; sturdy compressed paper containers; white paper towels, napkins; greaseproof (not waxed) paper | Quick heating or reheating Short-term cooking Generally not reusable |
| Wood and Basket Ware | Can eventually dry out and crack. Do not use painted, lacquered or varnished products. | Short-term reheating foods. |
| Aluminium Foil | Varying strengths and thickness used in small quantities only. NEVER cover food completely or allow foil to touch interior oven walls. | Shielding — protecting small areas of food from overcooking |
| Browning Dishes Crisper-Griddles | Dishes with metal composition or base coating preheated to produce extra high heat methods of cooking | Shallow pan frying/searing, browning; reheating pastries, roasts, etc. |
| Metal/Foil | Frozen cooked food containers should be shallow. Remove metal coated lids before use. Never allow metal to touch the interior oven walls. | Reheat |

| PLASTIC | COMMENTS | SUITABILITY |
|---|---|---|
| Cookware | Specially designed microwave cookware in varying qualities:<br>* lightweight, inexpensive for short-term use;<br>* durable, quality cookware for general use;<br>* high grade, durable containers with high heat capability designed for microwave and conventional ovens to withstand temperatures up to 200°C. | General microwave cookery to manufacturer's instructions |
| Cooking Pouches | Used in commercially prepared frozen foods. | Use according to pack instructions |
| Plastic Wrap | Choose only a microsafe or specially designed microwave product with high temperature tolerance and hot fat/oil resistance. | Covering foods |
| Freezer Bags | Do not use metal twist ties; allow for steam escape. | Defrosting or cooking |
| Oven Bags | Do not use metal twist ties; allow for steam escape. | Enclosed cooking |

DO NOT USE: Melamine ware, glued or cracked containers, crystal, narrow-necked jars or glasses.

# MICROWAVE COOKING TECHNIQUES

*Cod Pockets (page 40)*

*Successful microwave cooking depends upon an understanding of the principles and techniques involved. Some methods are used in conventional cooking as well, but they have a particular application in microwave cooking because of the special qualities of microwave energy.*

## FOOD QUANTITY, SIZE AND SHAPE

The smaller the amount, or the fewer the items, the less time the food will take to cook. Larger sizes or amounts take longer.

When altering recipe quantities, alter cooking times as follows:

● Allow 35–45% less time when halving ingredients;
● Allow 55–65% more time when doubling ingredients.

ALWAYS UNDERESTIMATE TIMES A LITTLE AND TEST BEFORE CONTINUING COOKING. It's always possible to add more cooking time but if you overcook nothing can be done to rectify the situation.

Uniformity of size and shape of foods is important — small evenly-shaped pieces cook faster and more evenly than larger irregular shapes. Careful arrangement of unevenly-shaped foods — larger or thicker pieces to the outer edges of containers and smaller or thinner sections in the centre — will assist in more even cooking.

Container size and shape affects cooking performance — foods placed in one layer in shallow dishes will cook more quickly than deeper multiple layers. Use recommended containers for best results.

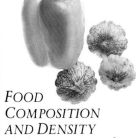

## FOOD COMPOSITION AND DENSITY

The basic structure of food — density, porosity, liquid content, etc. — is a factor that affects cooking or reheating times. Microwaves will take longer to penetrate tightly compacted or solid foods (meat roasts, fruit cakes, whole vegetables) than those that are open-textured or porous (minced meats, light cakes, breads and chopped vegetables).

Foods with high moisture content will take longer than drier foods. Foods with high levels of fat and sugar cook and reheat more rapidly to a higher temperature so need careful handling and testing when serving and eating.

Delicate ingredients and those with high protein content (meats, seafood, eggs, dairy foods, etc.) cook more successfully on lower power levels.

## STARTING TEMPERATURE

The colder the food, the more it will affect both cooking and / or reheating times — frozen and refrigerated foods need longer than those at room temperature. In taking starting temperature of foods into consideration any additional cooking times should be minimal so that foods will not be overcooked. Test, then continue cooking as required.

## ARRANGING FOOD

Microwave patterns within the oven provide greater concentration of energy around the outside areas and less in the centre. It is important that foods be placed to take full advantage of these patterns to ensure uniform cooking.

Place small dishes in a circle; individual food items around outer edges of container; one small

container (coffee cup) off-centre on turntable or oven base. Arrange larger, thicker foods outermost with smaller, thinner items in the centre; thickest sections of unevenly shaped foods facing outwards and thinner areas towards the centre. Separate food items to allow for microwave penetration from all sides. Rearrange food during cooking, as required.

Raising containers off the oven base or turntable has two advantages. It places foods closer to the energy source for quicker cooking and allows more microwave penetration from the reflected oven walls and base to enter the underside of the food for more even cooking. The use of a rack to lift roasting meats from the fats and juices in the baking dish is good nutritional practice.

During microwave cooking, stirring from outer edges to container centre, and vice versa, creates better distribution of heat. Foods that cannot be stirred may need turning or rotating to produce even cooking. Roast meats and other dense or bulky foods can be turned over or uneven shapes rotated. Food which cannot be disturbed may require a slight turn or alteration of position in the oven so that all microwave energy patterns are used.

## TIMING FOODS

Timing for microwave cooking is most important and critical for good results. Overcooking cannot be corrected, no matter what cooking method is used. Microwave oven wattages plus variations in food characteristics create differences in timing in recipes.

Cooking time guides and charts applicable to individual oven requirements are supplied in all the manufacturers' instruction manuals and recipe books and should be followed until

personal preferences require alteration. UNDERCOOK — TEST — ASSESS and continue cooking for best results.

**Standing Time**
Although microwave energy ceases the moment food is removed from the oven, contained heat within the food will continue to cook it further. Allowing food to stand — 20–30% of the cooking time — provides time for heat equalisation throughout the food, settling of juices in meats for better carving, and firming of consistency in cakes for easier handling.

Tight covering of foods during standing time will help retain heat longer, allowing for short time cooking of other foods and/or reheating. Loose covering on foods like roast meats prevents steam build-up for too moist surfaces.

## REHEATING FOODS

Heating of cooked foods is particularly successful in the microwave oven as foods retain colour, flavour and texture. The general techniques of rearranging, turning, stirring, covering, etc., should also be applied during reheating.

## PIERCING OR SLASHING FOODS

Many foods with naturally sealed skin or membrane surfaces (potatoes, egg yolks, whole fish, chicken livers, etc.) can develop considerable air expansion or steam pressure during cooking. To prevent possible splitting and/or bursting, several holes or slashes should be made with a skewer or knife point into the surface areas before cooking.

## BROWNING FOODS

Speedy microwave cooking does not allow sufficient time for natural browning of foods. Exceptions are meat roasts with fatty surfaces that cook for longer periods.

Browning aids for food include surface brushing with fats or oils, coloured glazes or sauces; sprinkling with seasonings or coloured or textured food additives; and applications of commercial products during cooking.

## COVERING FOODS

Using a covering when cooking foods prevents surface evaporation and traps steam both to retain moisture and assist in even heat distribution for quicker cooking. Coverings and their uses vary. Loose greaseproof paper prevents oven spatter. Container lids and plastic wrap retain moisture in foods; absorbent paper absorbs fat and/or steam.

Too tight or closely fitting covers should be avoided. They allow little space for expansion or escape of steam. When possible, do not allow plastic wrap to touch foods, especially those with high fat content.

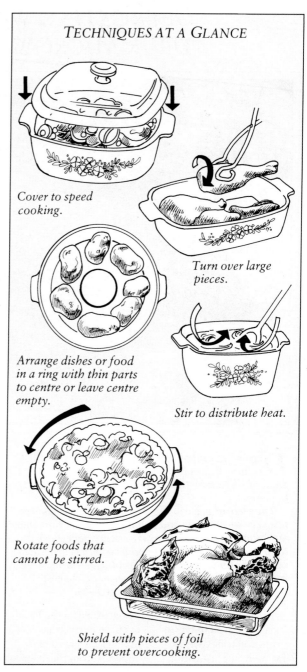

### TECHNIQUES AT A GLANCE

Cover to speed cooking.

Turn over large pieces.

Arrange dishes or food in a ring with thin parts to centre or leave centre empty.

Stir to distribute heat.

Rotate foods that cannot be stirred.

Shield with pieces of foil to prevent overcooking.

# DEFROSTING WITH YOUR MICROWAVE

*Soy and Honey Chicken (page 32)*

*D*efrosting or thawing is a process that slowly returns frozen food to its original state by gradually breaking the ice molecules, reducing them to water.

The Defrost cycle in the microwave oven achieves this very successfully and in a much shorter time than any other method. Microwave energy penetrates the food from the outer layers and heat that is generated within the outer molecules is conducted through the food, slowly thawing frozen areas. The Defrost setting on most microwave ovens is 30%.

Microwave ovens have improved in recent years and today we see far more sophistication being added to the basic oven. In defrosting manufacturers have added Automatic Weight Defrost, Pre-programmed Defrost, Compu Defrost, Sensor Defrost etc. Many of the manually set programs include an equivalent standing time for full defrosting. Large or dense foods may also require an additional standing time after defrosting to allow conduction of internal heat to fully reach the

16

centre or certain areas of the food not completely defrosted within the programmed time.

All methods of defrosting are explained in the instruction manual supplied with the microwave oven. It is important that the instruction manual or cookbook for each individual microwave oven be carefully read and followed. Most manufacturers of frozen convenience foods are now supplying instructions on packages for thawing and heating in a microwave oven. Compare these with the instructions supplied with the oven for wattage variances, e.g. 400–800 watts.

## MICROWAVE SHORTCUTS

**Melt chocolate.** Break into pieces, place in a dish and heat uncovered on 100% (High) power, checking every minute, until it can be stirred. Chocolate holds its shape until stirred so you can't tell that it has melted just by looking at it.

60g takes about 3 minutes to melt.

**Make croutons.** Melt 30g butter in a shallow dish, add 2 cups cubed bread and toss to coat on all sides. Spread out the cubes on a dish and heat on 100% (High) power for 4-5 minutes or until crisp and golden.

**Blanch almonds.** Heat 1 cup water in a dish on 100% (High) power until boiling. Add 1 cup shelled almonds, heat on 100% for 1 minute. Drain, slip skins off and spread almonds on absorbent paper to dry.

**Toast almonds.** Melt 1 tablespoon butter on a shallow dish, toss with ½ cup blanched almonds or ¼ cup slivered or flaked almonds. Heat on 100% (High) power, stirring every 2 minutes, until light golden brown. Stand for 5 minutes – the almonds will darken further on cooling.

**Toast sesame seeds.** Melt 1 tablespoon butter in a dish and stir in 3 tablespoons sesame seeds. Heat on 100% (High) power until light golden brown, stirring often. Drain on absorbent paper and stand for 2-3 minutes – the seeds will darken further on cooling.

## SHIELDING FOR EVEN DEFROSTING AND COOKING

*Defrosting: Feel meats during defrosting and shield warm areas which would start to cook before the end of defrosting. Before defrosting, place aluminium foil strip around sides of a casserole. Centre and sides of food will defrost evenly with energy absorbed from top to bottom.*

*Cooking: Shield loaf or square-shaped baked goods before cooking. Rearrange or remove foil after part of the cooking time. When cooking poultry, add foil sheets as needed to areas which appear to be cooking too fast (wing tips, etc.).*

## HOW TO DEFROST THICK ROASTS

*Unwrap roast. Place on rack in baking dish. Defrost for a quarter of the total time. Feel for warm areas; shield with aluminium foil. Turn meat over. Defrost for a second quarter of time.*

*Let stand 10 minutes. Continue to defrost, turning and shielding meat after each quarter of total time. Then let roast stand until a skewer can be inserted to the centre.*

## HOW TO DEFROST THIN ROASTS

*Set unwrapped meat on rack. Defrost for half time. Shield with foil; turn roast over.*

*Defrost remaining time. Let stand until meat can be pierced to the centre.*

### DEFROSTING HINTS AND TIPS

• When packaging a number of small items of foods together for freezing, separation sheets of greaseproof or plastic wrap should be used, e.g. for sausages, chops, steaks, fish fillets, etc. These may then be taken apart and placed in one layer on the defrosting dish, loosely covered, for more speedy thawing.

• Sections of bulk items such as minced or chopped meats, prawns, chicken pieces, etc., may be gradually broken away from the mass as the outside sections thaw, thus leaving a new frozen surface for further defrosting.

• The freezing of small quantities of some foods and those in shallow containers will allow for quicker defrosting results. One-cup portions of soups, sauces are recommended. These and other foods, frozen in microsafe containers, can also be defrosted and reheated more conveniently.

• Frozen poultry *must* be completely thawed before cooking, so that the cavity section can be thoroughly cleaned of certain bacteria which cause food spoilage. A final rinse out with hot water is recommended.

• Cooked sauces need vigorous whisking after defrosting to produce a smooth texture on reheating. Cream-style sauces that have been frozen for a long period can break down or separate during both defrosting and reheating.

• Home cooked or commercially prepared frozen pizzas are more successful if cooked on a pre-heated pizza or other browning dish without defrosting as the pastry or bread base can become tough and hard if a defrosting cycle is included.

• Pre-packaged frozen meats, chicken pieces, etc. on foam trays should be removed and placed on other dishes for defrosting.

• Bread slices or sandwiches, bread rolls, etc. may be quickly thawed in the microwave oven but timing is important to avoid a dry or powdered result. Small quantities are best placed between sheets of paper towel in a single layer and manually controlled at 100 or 70% power in 10 second bursts, turning the slices and towel over at least once. Serve the bread warm. Use appropriate fillings for sandwiches.

• For emergency morning/afternoon teas, etc., cook and freeze scones, biscuit slices or cakes, etc. in quantities with many separate portions. Remove portions required and

defrost on paper towels for a short period.

• It is more practical to freeze whole or layer cakes and then ice and decorate after defrosting.

• When defrosting home prepared plate dinners carefully remove food to another plate (room temperature) for speedier thawing and then reheating.

## STEP-BY-STEP DEFROSTING

• Remove foods from original freezer wrap or loosen as required, e.g. aluminium foil, plastic bags or film and rigid containers that are not microsafe. Discard any metal twists or clips. Follow package instructions for convenience foods.

• Place foods, preferably on a rack, in a shallow microsafe dish with sides to catch liquids from thawing foods.

• Defrost, loosely covered unless specifically stated otherwise, according to individual oven instructions.

• Where practical, large dense foods, meat joints, etc., may be turned over once or twice during defrosting to assist equal heat distribution.

• When defrost time is complete allow to stand as required. Continue specific food preparation and microwave cooking or reheating as required.

### DEFROSTING MEAT AND POULTRY

| CUT | MICROWAVE TIME | STANDING TIME |
|---|---|---|
| BEEF (Roast) | 8–10 minutes/500 g | 10–15 minutes |
| Steaks | 4–6 minutes/500 g | 5–10 minutes |
| Minced Beef | 5–8 minutes/500 g | 5–10 minutes |
| PORK (Roast) | 8–12 minutes/500 g | 10–15 minutes |
| Chops | 5–8 minutes/500 g | 5–10 minutes |
| Ribs | 6–8 minutes/500 g | 5–10 minutes |
| Minced Pork | 6–8 minutes/500 g | 5–10 minutes |
| LAMB (Roast) | 8–10 minutes/500 g | 10–15 minutes |
| Shoulder | 7–10 minutes/500 g | 10–15 minutes |
| Chops | 5–8 minutes/500 g | 5–10 minutes |
| POULTRY Turkey (Whole) | 6–10 minutes/500 g | 20–30 minutes |
| Buffe | 5–10 minutes/500 g | 15–20 minutes |
| Pieces | 7–10 minutes/500 g | 10–15 minutes |
| Chicken (Whole) | 5–8 minutes/500 g | 10–15 minutes |
| Pieces | 5–7 minutes/500 g | 10–15 minutes |
| Duck | 8–10 minutes/500 g | 10–15 minutes |

# MEAT

*Rosemary Lamb (page 23)*

*M*eat cookery by microwave employs most of the same practical knowledge and varied techniques of conventional meat cookery. Commonsense dictates that, depending on the cut of meat and its characteristics, you will dry roast, fry, braise or simmer in a microwave to serve up the desired results. You control those results simply by adding (or reducing) moisture, timing carefully and using the appropriate power levels. However, just as no single conventional method works best for all meats, neither will any single microwave method suit every cut, so check your manufacturer's instructions and pick the best applications to suit your needs from our recommendations. The weighing of meat in order to calculate cooking time is most important.

## ROASTING

Uniformly shaped joints cook more evenly than large, thick or odd-shaped ones. The fat content or presence of bone or stuffing will also affect cooking times.

Remember that microwaves penetrate food only by 2–3 cm; heat is then conducted towards the centre, just as in conventional cooking, so by controlling cooking times, you can achieve rare or medium results.

**Three Ways to Roast**
1 Place meat, fat side down, on microsafe rack in suitable roasting dish. This keeps it above fat and juices and improves flavour and appearance. (Be sure to remove fat and juices as they collect to reduce splattering and avoid a braised flavour.) Turn joint one to three times during cooking, depending on size and thickness, to help juices flow and keep meat moist. Brush occasionally with a prepared sauce to encourage browning.
2 Sear joint on all sides, using preheated browning dish, then reduce power level for remaining cooking time. While the roast stands, use the browning dish to bake vegetables or make gravy.
3 Use a combination of conventional and microwave methods for traditional taste and appearance. Sear meat in a pan on the range top and complete by microwave OR partially cook by microwave and complete in conventional oven. Suggested Power Level: Use 100% (High) power for 5–10 minutes, then reduce to 50–70% (Medium) power to finish cooking. The lower the power, the greater the moisture retention.

A meat thermometer will help you calculate the ideal cooking time. Use as the manufacturer directs. Only thermometers specially designed for microwaves can be used in the ovens during cooking. Regular thermometers must be kept outside the oven.

## POT ROASTING

This slow cooking, moist-heat method is ideal for the economical less tender meats. Use a browning dish, or a casserole on the range top, for initial searing. When converting conventional recipes, slightly reduce liquids and turn meat more frequently.

Suggested Power Level: after liquid is added, use 30–40% (Low) power; total cooking time will be reduced from the conventional by a quarter to a third.

## CASSEROLING

Cut meat and vegetables into uniform pieces. The cheaper, less tender meats will benefit from marinating. Cover surface of foods directly with microsafe wrap to submerge them in liquids, as exposed pieces will dehydrate and toughen. Stir occasionally to distribute the heat.

Suggested Power Level: use 30–40% (Low) power; total cooking times will be reduced by about a quarter.

## PAN-FRYING OR GRILLING

Chops, steaks, sausages and similar portions are well suited to this method. To sear, use pre-heated browning grill, platter or dish as manufacturer directs (or pre-sear conventionally on range top). Cook small quantities at a time and reheat browning dish between batches for the quickest, most evenly cooked results. Refer to oven manual or cookbooks for cooking times and power levels for various meats.

## OVEN BAG COOKERY

Oven bags are invaluable for cooking all less tender joints and pieces. Meats can be marinated and cooked in the same bag. Use as manufacturer directs. With oven mitts, carefully turn bag several times during cooking to mix the contents and distribute heat. *Never use metal ties to seal the bag.*

It is best not to

## MEAT ROASTING CHART

| FOOD | COOKING TIME | INSTRUCTIONS |
|---|---|---|
| BEEF | | |
| Rare | 10–12 minutes/500 g at 70% (Medium High) followed by 4–6 minutes/500 g at 50% (Medium) | Tie meat with string. Season with cracked pepper. Place fat side down on Low Rack. Turn over halfway through cooking. Stand 10–15 minutes before carving. |
| Medium | 7 minutes/500 g at 70% (Medium High) followed by 5–7 minutes at 50% (Medium) | |
| Well done | 8–10 minutes/500 g at 70% (Medium High) followed by 6–8 minutes at 50% (Medium) | |
| VEAL | | |
| Well done | 7–10 minutes/500 g at 70% (Medium High) | Tie meat with string. Place on a rack. Brush with melted butter. Turn over halfway through cooking. Stand 5–10 minutes before carving. |
| PORK | | |
| Well done | 8–10 minutes/500 g at 70% (Medium High) | Brush rind with oil and sprinkle with salt. Place on a rack. Turn over halfway through cooking. Stand 10–15 minutes before carving. |
| LAMB | | |
| Medium | 8–10 minutes/500 g at 70% (Medium High) | Season with 'Season All' or as desired. Place fat side down on a rack. Turn over halfway through cooking. Stand 10–15 minutes before carving. |
| Well done | 12–14 minutes/500 g at 70% (Medium High) | |

microwave beef topside in an oven bag as the result is dry tough meat.

## BASIC POINTS FOR MEAT COOKERY

- Fat: Remove the excess, but retain some to provide juice and flavour, and assist browning. If desired, cut away remainder after cooking.
- Salt: Don't use directly on meat surfaces: it draws out moisture, leaving tough, harsh-tasting areas. A little salt can be mixed into combinations (meat loaves, casseroles), if you like.
- Herbs: Use sparingly as they retain stronger flavour.
- Browning Aids: If desired, use liquid or powdered commercial browning agents, or a home-made sauce or glaze, to enhance colour.
- Marinades: Use before cooking to enhance flavour or tenderise tougher meat cuts.
- Aluminium Foil: Use foil strips or pieces to protect protruding or thinly fleshed sections of unevenly-shaped joints. Secure well; *do not*

*allow foil to touch oven floor or walls.* Use foil either during the initial or final half to one third of cooking time with equal results.

When testing shows meat to be almost cooked, remove from oven and loosely cover with a large sheet of foil. Stand joint for 10–20 minutes, depending on size, to let heat equalise, juices settle and flesh firm for easier carving.

A close, tight covering of foil over cooked meats will insulate and keep them hot briefly until the entire meal is ready for serving.

## Rosemary Lamb

*Preparation time:*
  15 minutes
*Cooking time:*
  1 hour + 20 minutes
  standing
*Serves* 4

1.25 kg leg of lamb
6 sprigs fresh (or 1 ½
  teaspoons dried)
  rosemary
1 teaspoon plain flour
3 tablespoons dry red
  wine
redcurrant jelly or mint
  sauce for serving

1  Pat lamb dry; trim off excess fat. Cut 6 slashes into fat layer; insert rosemary. Place lamb in oven cooking bag; knot end of bag closed. Pierce base of bag to allow juices to drain. Place on rack in microsafe baking dish.

2  Cook 30 minutes at 100% (High) power. For well-done meat, continue cooking at 50% (Medium) for 10 minutes, then at 100% for 20 minutes more. Lift bag, letting juices drain into dish; transfer to a plate and let stand *in bag* for 20 minutes before carving.

3  To make the gravy, place flour in small bowl; whisk in meat juices, scraping in any browned particles. Add wine. Cook at 100% power until thickened, 3 minutes, stirring once or twice (see Note).

4  To serve, open bag; drain any juices into gravy. Transfer lamb to heated serving plate. Carve and serve with gravy and jelly or mint sauce.

**Note:** This makes a small amount of concentrated gravy; dilute with a little hot stock if you want more.

# Chinese Beef and Vegetables

*Preparation time:*
  20 minutes
*Cooking time:*
  8 minutes + 8
  minutes standing time
*Serves* 4

½ *teaspoon ground*
  *ginger*
1 *clove garlic, crushed*
1 *tablespoon oil*
2 *teaspoons cornflour*
½ *cup water*
1 *tablespoon soy sauce*
1 *tablespoon hoisin or*
  *plum sauce*
500 *g rump steak, cut*
  *into thin strips*
2 *cups prepared*
  *vegetables (e.g. snow*
  *peas, broccoli florets,*
  *capsicum, carrot, onion)*

1  Use 100% (High) power throughout.
2  Place ginger, garlic and oil in a 2-litre casserole. Cook for 1 minute.
3  Blend cornflour with water until smooth. Stir in soy and hoisin sauces. Add to dish. Cook for 1 minute.
4  Mix in meat. Cover with plastic wrap. Cook for 4 minutes. Add vegetables. Cook for a further 3 minutes, stirring halfway through cooking.
5  Cover. Allow to stand for 3 minutes. Serve with boiled or fried rice.

*Chinese Beef and Vegetables*

*Sesame Pork*

# Sesame Pork

*Preparation time:*
  15 minutes + 2 hours
  marinating
*Cooking time:*
  14 minutes
*Serves* 4

4 *pork loin or*
  *forequarter chops*
  *(about 180 g each)*

2 *tablespoons soy sauce*
1 *teaspoon sugar*
2 *teaspoons freshly*
  *grated ginger or 1*
  *teaspoon powdered*
  *ginger*
*dash of Tabasco sauce*
1 *tablespoon oil*
2 *teaspoons sesame*
  *seeds*

1  Trim pork chops.
Combine soy, sugar,
ginger, Tabasco and oil.

Pour over pork. Allow
to marinate for 2 hours,
turn once.

2  Cook in microwave
dish on 100% power for
3 minutes. Turn, reduce
power to 50% and cook
for 8 minutes.

3  Sprinkle with sesame
seeds and cook a further
3 minutes on 50%
power. Stand 2 minutes
before serving.

*Rack of Lamb*

# Rack of Lamb

*Preparation time:*
  20 minutes
*Cooking time:*
  12 minutes + 5
  minutes standing
*Serves* 2

2 racks of lamb, each
  with 4 cutlets
1 clove garlic, slivered
1 large sprig fresh
  rosemary or ¼
  teaspoon dried
  rosemary

*freshly ground black
  pepper*

1  Use 100% (High)
power throughout.
2  Place the two racks
facing together with the
ends interlocking. Place
on a microsafe roasting
rack in a shallow 2-litre
casserole.
3  Cut small slits in the
surface of each joint.
Insert garlic slivers and
rosemary sprigs. Season
with pepper.
4  Cook for 10–12
minutes. Allow to stand,

covered with foil, for 5
minutes. Serve with a
platter of mixed
vegetables.
**Note:** Racks of lamb
vary considerably in
size. This recipe has been
tested using small racks.

26

# Chilli con Carne

*Preparation time:*
  30 minutes
*Cooking time:*
  23 minutes
*Serves 4*

1 tablespoon oil
1 large onion, finely
  chopped,
500 g minced steak
1 x 425 g can tomatoes
2 tablespoons tomato
  paste
1 teaspoon mild chilli
  powder
1 teaspoon paprika
1 teaspoon ground
  cumin
1 teaspoon ground
  coriander
*freshly ground black
  pepper*
1 x 440 g can red kidney
  beans, drained

1  Use 100% (High)
power throughout.
2  Place oil and onion in
a 3-litre casserole. Cover
with lid or plastic wrap.
Cook for 4 minutes.
3  Add mince. Mix well
with a fork. Cover.
Cook for 4 minutes.
4  Add tomatoes,
tomato paste, chilli
powder, paprika,
cumin, coriander and
pepper. Stir well. Cover.
Cook for 10 minutes,
stirring halfway through
cooking.
5  Add kidney beans to
mixture. Stir well. Cook
for 5 minutes. Serve
topped with a dollop of
yoghurt and
accompanied by a salad
and crusty bread.
Alternatively serve in
taco shells with tomato
and lettuce.

## HINT
Cook mince and
drain excess fat in one
step. Crumble mince
into a microsafe
colander over a
shallow baking dish.
The fat will drain into
the dish as the meat
cooks.

*Chilli con Carne*

# POULTRY

*Soy & Honey Chicken (p. 32), Tandoori Chicken with Cucumber Salad (p. 31)*

*P*oultry is ideal for microwave cooking. You can be assured of tender, juicy results, no matter what style of preparation you choose, and the saving on time is considerable. All types of poultry and poultry pieces can be cooked most successfully following this guide.

Chicken: The whole bird and all of its parts, on or off the bone, are perfect for microwaving, including minced raw chicken.

Duck: The whole or sectioned bird microwaves well, but avoid larger, older or very fatty ducks.

Turkey: The small whole bird (4 kg or less), turkey fillets and whole breasts are best for fast roasting. Thigh or leg portions benefit from slower, moist cooking at low power levels, but offer little saving in cooking time.

Game Birds: For best results, all game birds should be cooked slowly at low power levels.

Prepared Poultry: Birds ready-prepared (boned and rolled, meat loaves, crumbed portions) should be microwaved following packet instructions or after reference to supplier or processor.

## PREPARING THE WHOLE BIRD

● Fully thaw, if frozen, and clean the cavity. If necessary, rinse well, drain and thoroughly dry.

● Stuff bird loosely (or place fresh herbs, celery and quartered lemon or onion in cavity). As short cooking times for most poultry may not be sufficient to thoroughly cook raw stuffings, be sure to pre-cook perishable ingredients (bacon, minced meat) before mixing with breadcrumbs and seasonings. And, if using dried herbs, reconstitute in a little hot water before adding. Stuffings can also be microwaved and served separately if you prefer.

● Truss or tie wings and legs to body to prevent them touching oven walls.

● Place bird, breast down, on microsafe roasting rack in dish to raise it above cooking juices.

● Brush all over with home-made or commercial glaze for added colour (soy sauce or other savoury sauce, chutney, honey or jam, butter or oil, and unsalted seasonings).

● If desired, use small pieces of foil to shield legs, wing tips or breast. Secure with toothpicks, making sure foil does not touch oven walls. Remove foil one-third to halfway through cooking time for best results.

## ROASTING

● Use 100% power for 5–10 minutes; then reduce to lower power to finish (use 70% power for smaller birds; 50% power for larger). Check timing in oven manual or cookbooks. Be sure to calculate cooking time for stuffed birds on weight *after* stuffing.

● Turn bird one to three times during cooking. *Turn chickens once, ducks twice and turkeys three times.* Readjust or remove foil, and apply glaze as needed. Cover bird loosely with greased baking paper to help even the cooking and prevent spattering; remove near the end of cooking time.

● Drain excess fats and cooking juices as they accumulate; this helps shorten cooking time and reduce spatter.

● Remove bird from oven when almost cooked, when juices begin to run clear and leg joints move easily in their sockets.

● Remove bird to serving platter; loosely cover with foil and stand for 10 minutes. This allows for even heat distribution so the bird finishes cooking evenly and lets the juices settle for easier carving. Use this time to finish cooking the vegetables or make the gravy.

## COOKING POULTRY PIECES

• Arrange pieces in single layer in microsafe dish with thicker sections towards the outside.

• Glaze, if desired, and loosely cover.

• Cook at 70–100% power for required time, turning or rearranging pieces once or twice.

## OVEN BAG COOKERY

Whole birds and portions (especially the large or less tender) microwave beautifully with a little liquid and seasonings in plastic oven bags. Use bags as manufacturer directs, but we recommend you slightly reduce the flour in the bag to 2–3 teaspoons. You can marinate birds in the same cooking bag for convenience.

## CASSEROLE COOKERY

Pre-sear, part or fully cook the bird as recipe requires. Use 100% power the first 5–7 minutes; then reduce to 50% power. For even cooking, stir and rearrange large pieces, and cover dish with lid or microsafe plastic wrap to trap steam.

• Layered casserole combinations which cannot be stirred should be elevated on an upturned dessert or pie plate, and cooked a little longer and at a lower power setting to provide greater microwave penetration for better heat distribution.

## FAT-FREE COOKING

Chicken: Remove most of the skin and fat, but not all of it, before cooking. Some fat juices

## POULTRY ROASTING CHART

| POULTRY | COOKING TIME | INSTRUCTIONS |
|---|---|---|
| CHICKEN Whole | 10–12 minutes/500 g at 70% (Medium High) | Brush with melted butter. Season as desired. Place chicken breast-side down on a rack. Turn over and shield wings and legs halfway through cooking. Stand 10–15 minutes before carving. |
| Pieces | 8–10 minutes/500 g at 70% (Medium High) | Season as desired. Place chicken skin-side down on a rack. Turn over halfway through cooking. |
| TURKEY Whole | 15–18 minutes/500 g at 50% (Medium) | Truss turkey. Place breast-side down on a rack. Turn over halfway through cooking and shield wings and legs. Baste with melted butter 2–3 times during cooking. Stand 10–15 minutes before carving. |
| Buffe | 12–15 minutes/500 g at 50% (Medium) | Place breast-side down on a rack. Turn over halfway through cooking and shield wings and legs. Baste with melted butter 2–3 times during cooking. Stand 10–15 minutes before carving. |
| DUCK | 10 minutes on 100% (High) followed by 7–10 minutes/ 500 g at 50% (Medium) | Place duck breast-side down on a rack. Pierce skin to drain excess fat. Turn over halfway through cooking. Stand 10–15 minutes before carving. |

are needed to prevent dry, stringy flesh, especially where meat only thinly covers the bones. To balance the absence of fat, try marinating in a low-fat marinade and/or cooking in an oven bag. If you prefer the skin intact, be sure to use a roasting rack and remove fat during cooking as it collects below.

Duck: Pierce skin all over and score very fatty areas with a knife to release excess fat. Always roast on a rack and remove fat drippings as they collect.

Self-basting Turkey and Chicken: During cooking, pierce the skin each time the bird is turned to release fat.

## REHEATING COOKED POULTRY

To avoid dry or tough results, add a little moisture and tightly cover. Microwave sliced poultry at 70% power; larger pieces at 50% power, turning where possible for even heat distribution.

# Tandoori Chicken with Cucumber Salad

*Preparation time:*
  15 minutes
*Cooking time:*
  9 minutes + 10
  minutes standing
*Serves 2*

4 *chicken thighs on the bone, about 125 g each, skins removed*
4 *tablespoons yoghurt*
1 *clove garlic, crushed*
1 *tablespoon tomato paste*
1 *teaspoon turmeric*
1 *teaspoon garam masala*
1 *teaspoon crushed coriander seeds*
*ground pepper*
2 *teaspoons cornflour (optional; see Note)*

Salad
½ *unpeeled cucumber*
1 *teaspoon salt*
1 *small onion, thinly sliced*
2 *tablespoons vegetable oil*
2 *teaspoons white vinegar*
½ *teaspoon coriander seeds*

1  Use 100% (High) power throughout.
2  Make 3 slashes in meat of each thigh with sharp knife. Arrange, spoke fashion, in shallow, microsafe dish. Combine yoghurt,

garlic, tomato paste, spices and pepper; spoon over chicken.
3  Cover; cook for 5 minutes. Turn and rearrange thighs; cover and cook 4 minutes more. Stand for 10 minutes (see Note).
4  To make the Salad, score and thinly slice cucumber, sprinkle with salt and let stand for 10 minutes. Rinse and drain well; toss with onion in serving dish.
5  Whisk together oil, vinegar, coriander seeds and extra pepper to taste; pour over salad. Serve with chicken.
**Note:** If sauce is thin, transfer chicken to heated serving plates and pour cooking juices into microsafe jug. Blend cornflour with a little cold water; stir into juices. Cook 1½ minutes, stirring once or twice, until thickened. Pour over chicken.

---

HINT
Large poultry will brown well in the microwave oven because it takes longer to cook, and many birds are self-basting. Small birds may need basting, and bottled browning sauces and seasoning powders are also very successful.

---

# Soy and Honey Chicken

*Preparation time:*
15 minutes
*Cooking time:*
35 minutes
*Serves* 4

30 g butter
1 tablespoon soy sauce
1 tablespoon honey
1 teaspoon dried parsley
  flakes
1 x 1.5 kg chicken

1  Combine butter, soy, honey and parsley in a small microsafe bowl, cover and cook on 100% power for 1 minute.
2  Brush soy and honey mixture all over chicken. Place chicken breast-side down on a microwave roasting rack in a dish. Cook on 100% power for 15 minutes, basting with soy and honey mixture. Turn chicken over; cook a further 20 minutes on 70% power.
3  Stand chicken, covered, for 10 minutes before serving.

> **HINT**
> Poultry can be partly cooked in the microwave oven and finished in a conventional oven for a traditional roast dinner treat.

# Turkey Slices with Orange Cream Sauce

*Preparation time:*
20 minutes
*Cooking time:*
30 minutes
*Serves* 4

4 turkey fillets
¼ cup plain flour
1 teaspoon dry mustard
  powder
3 tablespoons milk
1 tablespoon olive oil
2 tablespoons butter,
  melted
3 small oranges
2 tablespoons brandy
2 teaspoons cornflour
½ cup cream

1  Rub the turkey fillets all over with combined flour and mustard; dip both sides in the milk, then again lightly coat with flour — this forms a thin batter coating.
2  Preheat a microware browning dish for 6–7 minutes; quickly brush some butter and oil mixture over and add the turkey fillets, pressing down onto hot surface to sear all over.
3  Turn the fillets, adding a little more butter and oil; return dish to the oven and cook on 100% (High) power for 3–4 minutes.
4  Decrease setting to 30% (Defrost) and continue cooking, turning fillets occasionally, for 12–17 minutes until the meat is cooked through; lift fillets onto a heated serving dish and cover to retain heat.
5  Meanwhile, cut rind of 1 orange into thin shreds and squeeze juice from oranges. Add juice and brandy to the browning dish and scrape sediments in the dish with a plastic spatula.
6  Cook on 100% (High) power, stirring frequently, for 3 minutes. Swirl the blended cream through, and when sauce is bubbling and thickened, add the orange shreds and spoon over the turkey fillets. Serve immediately.

> **HINT**
> Poultry needs to be trussed correctly for roasting to prevent protruding wings and legs from overcooking and drying out in the oven. Similarly the bird should be elevated in the dish by means of a rack or upturned small plate to allow for all round cooking, even though it is suggested that occasional turning will also achieve this result.

*Turkey Slices with Orange Cream Sauce*

## Chicken Liver Pâté

*Preparation time:*
  40 minutes + setting
  time
*Cooking time:* nil
*Serves* 4

250 g butter
500 g chicken livers,
  washed, trimmed and
  chopped
1 onion, chopped
1 or 2 cloves garlic,
  crushed
1½ tablespoons dry
  sherry
seasonings to taste
3 tablespoons chopped
  green olives
2 or 3 stuffed green
  olives, extra

Melba Toast
8 thin slices bread

1  Use 100% (High)
power throughout.
2  Place 180 g butter in a
microsafe bowl. Cook
for 1½–2 minutes. Add
livers, onion and garlic.
Cover with plastic wrap.
Cook for 3–4 minutes.
Stir halfway through
cooking.

3  Stir in sherry and
seasonings. Cover. Cook
for 3 minutes. Stir well.
Allow to cool.
4  Spoon mixture into a
food processor or
blender. Process until
smooth. Mix in olives.
Spoon into one large or
two smaller serving
dishes. Refrigerate until
firm.
5  Slice extra olives
thinly. Place decoratively
on top of pâté. Place
remaining butter in a
small microsafe bowl.
Cook for 45–60
seconds. Spoon over
pâté. Leave any
sediment in bowl.
Refrigerate until set.
Serve with Melba Toast
or toasted French loaf.
6  To prepare Melba
Toast, remove crusts
from bread slices. Roll
out with a rolling pin
until flat and compact.
Slice into quarters
diagonally. Place on an
oven tray. Bake in a
moderate oven (180°C)
until crisp, browned and
just beginning to curl.

*Chicken Liver Pâté*

## Chicken Breasts in Almond Sauce

*Preparation time:*
  15 minutes
*Cooking time:*
  22 minutes
*Serves* 4

4 chicken breast fillets
1 tablespoon lemon juice
freshly ground black
  pepper
1 onion, sliced
30 g butter
½ cup chicken stock
½ cup white wine
1 tablespoon cornflour
½ cup almond flakes
½ cup sour cream

1  Trim the chicken
breasts, brush with
lemon juice and place in
a greased microsafe dish.
2  Sprinkle with pepper
and cover with onion
slices and pieces of
butter; cover and cook
on 70% for 10–12
minutes.
3  Lift chicken and onion
pieces onto another dish,
cover, and set aside. Stir
blended stock, wine and
cornflour into the dish
juices and cook on 70%
for 2 minutes, stirring
two or three times.
4  Add almonds to the
sauce and swirl the sour
cream through; return
chicken and onions,
spooning the sauce over
all. Heat through on
50% for 6–8 minutes.
5  Serve with fresh
seasonal vegetables.

*Chicken Breasts in Almond Sauce*

# FISH AND SHELLFISH

*Salmon with Lime Mayonnaise (page 38)*

*Fresh and frozen fish are tender, flaky and retain moisture and flavour when cooked in the microwave. As fish have very fragile connective tissue and normally cook quickly by any method, careful timing and testing when microwaving is crucial — just a little overcooking can result in dryness and loss of delicate texture.*

*With a microwave oven, you can steam, bake or shallow fry, using the minimum of oil. Deep frying is not recommended.*

*Fish continues to cook briefly after microwaving. When testing for doneness, you must allow for this and test shortly before the end of the allotted cooking time.*

*Fish is sufficiently cooked when its flesh begins to whiten and flakes with only a little resistance when tested at thickest part. Serve thin fillets from this stage immediately; by the time they reach the table, they will have finished cooking. To help thicker fish cuts or whole fish finish cooking most evenly, be sure to tightly cover and stand 1–2 minutes before serving.*

*Shellfish is cooked when its transparent flesh turns white and the shell, depending on variety, changes colour to orange-red.*

and fins with pieces of foil during first half of cooking time. *Remember: foil must not touch oven walls!* Cut through skin and flesh at the thickest part in several places to a depth of 2 mm to prevent splitting and shrinkage, and help even the cooking.

Cook stuffing ingredients (onion, bacon) before placing in the fish cavity as the short cooking times required for the fish may not be sufficient to thoroughly cook raw stuffings.

## FISH FILLETS
Arrange in cooking container with tail ends folded under to give a uniform thickness. Alternatively, protect thinnest ends with foil strips for half the cooking time. Arrange thickest ends towards the outside of the cooking container and rearrange during cooking, if necessary. Cover with microsafe plastic wrap. This both hastens cooking time and prevents dryness.

For thin to medium-thick fillets: Cook at 100% (High) power and serve at once.

Commercially frozen fillets: Follow packet cooking instructions for times and power settings. *Undercook first*, test, then continue cooking, if required.

## WHOLE FISH
For whole fish, thick fillets, steaks or cutlets, cook at 70% (Medium-High) power, test, and then briefly stand before serving.

Remove eyes, or pierce them at the side, to prevent steam build-up. Cover thin tail end

## SHELLFISH
*Do not place live shellfish in the microwave oven!* Kill first by drowning in fresh water, or by freezing 2–3 hours.

Shellfish can be cooked with shells intact, as microwaves pass through to the flesh inside. Tie legs of lobster, crayfish and crabs to their bodies. Use foil to shield thin sections. Regularly stir or turn small shellfish (such as prawns) for even cooking.

Choose a lower power setting (about 70%) when cooking scallops, squid and cuttlefish, and cover with a lid or sauce. The high moisture content of their flesh can cause 'popping' if cooked at higher power levels.

To open oysters: Heat at 100% (High) power for 30–60 seconds, depending on the quantity.

To open mussels: Proceed as for oysters, removing each shell from cooking container as it opens. Those which resist opening should be opened by hand, but tested for freshness (appearance and odour) before serving.

## CURED AND PREPARED FISH

**Cold-smoked and salted fish**: Depending on the smoking or salting process, soak or rinse fish well before cooking, and cook in liquids for best results.

**Canned seafood**: Use in entrées with sauce, combination casseroles or mixed with other ingredients for best results. Most varieties of canned seafood reheat extremely well.

**Crumbed seafood**: Use a browning dish to cook commercially frozen or freshly prepared seafood with crumb coatings. Preheat dish no longer than 5–6 minutes and oil the dish only when cooking home-prepared seafood, as commercially crumbed products contain sufficient fat.

## DEFROSTING FISH

Remove from freezer wrapping and place on a rack inside a casserole to raise it above any collecting juices. For best results, *only partially defrost* fish in the microwave, and then let stand at room temperature to thaw completely. Over-defrosting by microwave can start the cooking process in the thinner sections.

Separate pieces from large portions and set aside as they thaw. Keep refrigerated until all pieces are ready to cook. Pat fish dry with paper towels before cooking. Reserve any thawed juices and use them in sauces, if desired.

## REHEATING COOKED FISH

Cover dish loosely and reheat at 50–70% power for the shortest possible time, as the delicate texture of fish can be quickly destroyed. For fish served with sauce, reheat each separately where possible and combine before serving.

# Salmon with Lime Mayonnaise

*Preparation time:*
25 minutes
*Cooking time:*
13 minutes
*Serves* 4

2 tablespoons white wine
2 tablespoons white wine vinegar
3 peppercorns
1 small bay leaf
4 salmon or ocean trout cutlets, about 250 g each
juice of 1 lime
3 egg yolks
seasonings to taste
150 g butter, cut into pieces

1  Use 100% (High) power throughout.
2  Place wine, vinegar, peppercorns and bay leaf in a 1-litre casserole. Cook for 3 minutes. Strain. Reserve liquid.
3  Place salmon on a large microsafe platter. Ensure that the thickest part of each cutlet faces the outside edge of the platter. Drizzle with lime juice. Cover with plastic wrap.
4  Cook for 6–8 minutes. Drain off juices. Reserve. Keep salmon covered. Set aside.
5  Whisk egg yolks with reserved vinegar mixture in a 4-cup jug. Beat in

juices from fish and seasonings. Cook for 1 minute.

6 Place butter in a 2-cup jug. Cook for 30–60 seconds or until melted. Gradually whisk butter into egg yolk mixture. Return to microwave to reheat for 15–30 seconds. Whisk every 10 seconds.

7 Transfer salmon to serving plates. Top with sauce. Garnish with fresh chervil. Serve with baby new potatoes, carrots and snow peas.

## Oysters Kilpatrick

*Preparation time:*
  *20 minutes*
*Cooking time:*
  *4 minutes*
*Serves 2*

*2 rashers rindless bacon, chopped*
*1 tablespoon Worcestershire sauce*
*1 tablespoon lemon juice*
*freshly ground black pepper*
*12 oysters on the shell*

1 Use 100% (High) power throughout.

2 Combine bacon, sauce, juice and pepper in a small microsafe bowl. Cover with plastic wrap. Cook for 2–2½ minutes.

3 Place oysters on a microsafe dinner plate in a circular pattern. Sprinkle with bacon mixture.

4 Cook for 1–1½ minutes. Serve on a bed of rock salt with lemon or lime wedges.

*Oysters Kilpatrick*

# Creamy Baked Mussels

*Preparation time:*
   30 minutes
*Cooking time:*
   18 minutes
*Serves* 4

2 kg green lip (New
   Zealand) mussels,
   beards removed and
   scrubbed (see Note)
30 g butter
1 large onion, finely
   chopped
2 cloves garlic, crushed
150 mL dry white wine
freshly ground black
   pepper
2 egg yolks
½ cup cream
1 tablespoon chopped
   parsley

1  Prepare mussels. Use a small knife to remove beards (you may not find one on every mussel).
2  Place butter in a 5-litre casserole. Cook on 100% (High) power for 30–40 seconds. Add onion and garlic. Mix well. Cook on 100% for 4–5 minutes.
3  Stir in wine and seasonings. Add mussels. Cover with lid or plastic wrap. Cook on 100% for 8–10 minutes.
4  Spoon mussels into serving bowls with a slotted spoon. Blend egg yolks and cream into liquid in dish. Cook on 70% (Medium High) for 2–3 minutes, stirring halfway through cooking.
5  Spoon sauce over mussels. Sprinkle with parsley. Serve with crusty bread and salad.

**Note:** New Zealand mussels are always open when purchased as they must be steamed before they are sold. If you use the smaller variety, discard any that do not open after cooking.

# Cod Pockets

*Preparation time:*
   20 minutes
*Cooking time:*
   12 minutes
*Serves* 4

4 cod steaks, about
   150 g each
seasonings to taste
1 lemon, thinly sliced
3 tomatoes, peeled and
   sliced
1 small onion, thinly
   sliced
4 tablespoons dry white
   wine
1 tablespoon chopped
   fresh mint
12 capers
12 black olives

1  Use 100% (High) power throughout.
2  Cut 16 x 20 cm squares of greaseproof paper. Place each fish steak on one double square of paper. Sprinkle with seasonings.
3  Arrange lemon slices over fish. Top with tomato and onion. Spoon 1 tablespoon wine over each fish.
4  Sprinkle each fish steak with mint. Top with capers and olives. Place double squares of paper over fish. Fold edges of paper together to seal.
5  Place parcels on a large flat plate. Cook for 10–12 minutes.
6  Place parcels on serving plates. Snip open the paper. Peel back like petals. Garnish with sprigs of fresh mint. Serve with a tossed green salad and crusty bread.

---

### HINT
Butter, margarine or a little oil can be added to the dish when cooking fish but this is not entirely necessary — covering will assist in retaining any steam and help to keep the fish moist.

*Creamy Baked Mussels, Cod Pockets*

# EGGS AND DAIRY FOODS

*Speedy Spanish Omelette (page 44), Eggs Florentine (page 45)*

*Two very basic but important rules apply to cooking eggs or dairy products in the microwave (indeed by any cooking method): use low heat and always undercook.*

*Few foods are more convenient or economical than eggs, and when it comes to cooking them nothing is faster than the microwave oven. But, because it is so quick, it can prove to be a delicate operation where timing is of the utmost importance.*

*As with most foods, eggs will continue to cook after being removed from the microwave oven so time must be allowed for this in order to avoid the risk of tough or rubbery scrambled eggs or omelettes, and overcooked or hardened poached or baked eggs. Even 20–30 seconds can make all the difference.*

*To help in avoiding overcooking, we recommend that eggs be cooked on 50% (Medium) power or even less, unless they are incorporated with other foods which may require a different procedure.*

*Egg yolks contain more fat than the whites, so will reach a higher temperature and therefore cook more quickly. Careful puncturing of the membrane enclosing the yolk contents will help to avoid a build-up of too much pressure resulting in exploding, particularly in fried, poached or baked eggs.*

containing milk, cheese and light-coloured meats or fish, sprinkle the surface with paprika, seasoned pepper or cayenne before cooking. After cooking, fresh chopped parsley, chives etc. may be used.

Cooked custard sauces are simple to make in the microwave oven but should also be cooked on Medium setting, stirring frequently so that they will not curdle, separate or become lumpy, depending on the added ingredients. Cover on standing to prevent a skin forming over the surface.

## DAIRY FOODS

Milk and other dairy foods play such an important role in all manner of foods that it is inevitable that they will be used often for microwave cookery. Milk heats easily to scald or boiling point but if stirred halfway through the heating time, the surface tension breaks, which prevents the heated liquid under the covering skin from erupting. Careful watching is also necessary to prevent a boil-over. For safety, and to prevent a possible scorched taste, use a Low setting.

Cheese is sensitive to too high a heat. Too long in the cooking process will cause the high protein content to toughen, so heat on a Medium or Low setting for a short time only. If using to create a topping on casseroles, add towards the end of time.

The best cheeses to use for melting are natural and processed Cheddar and mozzarella. Where more taste is needed use Parmesan or similar dry-texture, mature cheese.

For added colour to the surface of casseroles

## EGGS

**Boiling:** Eggs in the shell boiled conventionally require less work on your part. If using a microwave-designed egg boiler, follow manufacturer's instructions.

**Poaching:** Place 2 tablespoons water in a small microsafe dish or ramekin. Cover with microsafe plastic wrap. Heat at 100% power until boiling.

Carefully crack eggs into water; pierce the

yolks. Re-cover and cook until white is almost cooked, 30 seconds more. Stand, covered, 1 minute more or until set to your liking.

**Scrambling:** Place 1 teaspoon butter in microsafe dish; cook at 100% power until melted, and then swirl butter over base and sides. Add 2 eggs beaten with 2 tablespoons water, season to taste. Cover and cook 45 seconds. Stir well; cover and cook at 50% (Medium) power 45 seconds more. Stir again; serve with chopped parsley.

Chopped ham or ½ cup grated cheese can be added. Cook at 100% power for 2 minutes; stir and cook 1 minute more. Stand 1 or 2 minutes before serving.

**Omelette:** Lightly grease a shallow, microsafe pie dish. Add 4 sliced mushrooms. Cover; cook at 100% power for 1½ minutes. Lightly beat 3 eggs with 3 tablespoons water; season to taste and pour over mushrooms. Cook at 50% power for 2½ minutes, stirring several times. Sprinkle with ½ cup grated cheese; fold omelette in half and serve at once.

**Baked Egg Custard:** Heat 500 mL milk in large bowl at 70% power for about 1 minute. Beat 3 eggs with 3 tablespoons caster sugar and ½ teaspoon imitation vanilla essence; pour into milk, mix well. Divide mixture between 4 custard cups. Sprinkle with nutmeg. Arrange in a circle in microwave. Cook at 50% power for 8 minutes. Quarter-turn custards twice and rearrange once during cooking. Stand 10 minutes, then serve.

## MILK-BASED SAUCES

For a basic, thin white sauce, heat 1 tablespoon butter at 100% power for 1 minute. Add 1 tablespoon flour, salt and freshly ground pepper and stir well. Cook 10–15 seconds and stir again. Whisk in 1 cup of milk until well-blended. Cook, uncovered, 1 minute; stir well. Cook 2 minutes more, or until smooth and bubbling, stirring two or three times. For a medium white sauce, use 2 tablespoons *each* butter and flour; for a thick white sauce, use 3 tablespoons butter and 4 tablespoons flour and use for binding croquette mixtures.

To turn a white sauce into a mornay, stir ½–1 cup grated cheese (processed or natural tasty) into sauce after cooking. Stir until melted. Reheat if necessary at 30% (Low) power for 30 seconds.

## Speedy Spanish Omelette

*Preparation time:*
15 minutes
*Cooking time:*
8 minutes
*Serves 2*

1 tablespoon oil
15 g butter
1 small onion, chopped
1 small potato, peeled and sliced
½ each green and red capsicum, seeded and cut into strips
60 g button mushrooms, sliced
4 eggs
seasoning

1 Use 100% (High) power throughout.
2 Place oil and butter in a shallow 20 cm microsafe dish. Cook 1 minute.
3 Add onion and potato. Cover with plastic wrap. Cook for 3 minutes, stirring once.

4  Stir in capsicum and mushrooms. Cover again. Cook for 2 minutes, stirring once.
5  Beat eggs with seasoning. Pour over vegetables. Cover. Cook for 2 minutes.
6  If there is any uncooked egg, use a fork to draw the mixture from the sides into the middle while tilting the dish to allow the uncooked mixture to run to the edges. Cook uncovered for 1–2 minutes or until lightly set.
7  Cut into quarters. Serve with a tossed green salad and crusty bread.
**Hint:** For a fluffy, soufflé-type omelette, separate eggs. Beat whites until soft peaks form. Fold in yolks and cooked vegetable mixture. Cook on 30% (Defrost) for 7–8 minutes or until set.

**HINT**
Egg and cheese dishes, milk and other high protein foods tend to toughen when cooked on too high a power — 70% or 50% will produce a better result, depending on amount, recipe and cooking time.

## Eggs Florentine

*Preparation time:*
   20 minutes
*Cooking time:*
   17 minutes
*Serves 2*

2 *large potatoes, scrubbed*
250 *g packet frozen spinach*
30 *g butter or margarine*
½ *teaspoon nutmeg seasoning*
2 *eggs*
*paprika*

1  Use 100% (High) power throughout.
2  Prick potatoes all over with a fork. Place on a microsafe plate. Cook for 10 minutes or until tender.
3  Place spinach in a microsafe bowl. Cover with plastic wrap. Cook for 5 minutes, stirring once, until thawed. Squeeze out any excess water.
4  Slice the top off each potato. Carefully scoop out the cooked flesh with a spoon. Leave a shell about 1 cm thick inside the skin.
5  Add potato to spinach. Mix in butter, nutmeg and seasonings. Spoon mixture into potato shells. (Refrigerate any excess filling and reheat with a little butter as a meal accompaniment.) Leave

a hollow in the centre of each.
6  Break an egg into each hollow. Pierce yolks carefully with a toothpick (see Note).
7  Place potatoes on plate. Cover with plastic wrap. Cook for 1–2 minutes, or until egg white is just set. Sprinkle with paprika. Serve with lettuce leaves and tomato wedges.
**Note:** When piercing egg yolks you need only make the tiniest hole in the outer membrane so that the yolk does not burst on cooking. If you make too large a hole the egg will appear broken when cooked.

**HINT**
Melting butter by microwave is obviously simple. Its best application is for clarified butter (ghee): simply pour off the clear butter oil from milk solids and store for cooking. Although frying is generally not recommended in the microwave, clarified butter can be used with a browning dish to give potatoes and the like good colour and crispness.

# Queen of Puddings

*Preparation time:*
  20 minutes
*Cooking time:*
  8 minutes
*Serves* 4

4 *cups roughly chopped*
  *sponge finger biscuits*
  *(about 125 g)*
2 *egg yolks*
150 *mL milk*
6 *tablespoons raspberry*
  *jam*

Creamy Vanilla Custard
2 *eggs*
5 *teaspoons caster sugar*
2 *teaspoons cornflour*
150 *mL milk*
150 *mL cream*
¹/₂ *teaspoon imitation*
  *vanilla essence*

Meringue Topping
2 *egg whites*
¹/₃ *cup caster sugar*

1  Use 100% (High) power throughout.
2  Place sponge biscuits in the base of a microsafe and ovenproof casserole. Combine egg yolks and milk. Pour over biscuits. Spoon over jam. Level top. Set aside.
3  To prepare Custard, whisk eggs, sugar and cornflour together in a small bowl. Heat milk and cream in a microsafe jug for 1½–2 minutes. Gradually whisk into egg mixture.
4  Return egg mixture to jug. Cook for 2–2½ minutes, stirring every 30 seconds, until custard is thickened. Stir in vanilla. Set aside.
5  To prepare Meringue, beat egg whites until stiff. Add sugar, 1 tablespoon at a time, beating until thick, smooth and glossy.
6  Spoon over soaked biscuits and jam. Swirl with a fork. Cook for 2½–3 minutes or until well risen. Brown pudding under a preheated grill.
7  Reheat custard for 30–60 seconds. Serve with pudding.

# Fruit Roly-Poly with Orange Cream

*Preparation time:*
40 minutes
*Cooking time:*
7 minutes
*Serves 6*

1 cup chopped dried
apricots
¾ cup chopped pitted
dates
⅓ cup raisins
rind of 1 orange
¼ cup sugar
2 cups self-raising flour,
sifted
125 g butter, at room
temperature
2–3 tablespoons water

Orange Cream
2 egg yolks
1 egg
½ teaspoon cornflour
5 teaspoons caster sugar
juice of 1 orange
150 mL milk

1  Use 100% (High) power throughout.
2  Mix apricots, dates, raisins, half the orange rind and half the sugar together in a mixing bowl. Reserve 4 tablespoons of this mixture for decoration.
3  Combine flour, butter and remaining sugar and orange rind in a bowl. Stir in water, adding a little extra if required to mix to a soft dough.
4  Knead lightly. Roll out to a 28 cm square on a lightly floured surface or between 2 sheets of plastic wrap. Spoon fruit mixture over top.
5  Brush pastry edges with water. Roll up as a Swiss roll. Wrap loosely in greaseproof paper, twisting the ends. Place seam-side down on a large flat plate. Cook for 5–7 minutes. Stand for 5 minutes.
6  To prepare Orange Cream, mix egg yolks, egg, cornflour and sugar in a small bowl. Whisk in orange juice and milk. Cook for 3–4 minutes, whisking every 30 seconds until thick.
7  Unwrap roly-poly. Transfer to a serving plate. Spoon reserved fruit on top. Serve sliced with Orange Cream.

*Queen of Puddings, Fruit Roly-Poly with Orange Cream*

# RICE AND PASTA

*Tagliatelle with Spinach (page 50), Vegetable Biryani (page 50)*

*R*ice, *like most whole-grain cereals, needs time to absorb moisture and rehydrate, so for this reason there is little time saved by cooking it in a microwave oven as compared with conventional cooking methods. But the results — separate, fluffy grains with no sticky, gluggy lumps — are certainly more predictable and you will have the advantage of no messy saucepans. Rice can be cooked, served, refrigerated or frozen and reheated all in the one dish without fear of losing its appearance, taste and texture.*

The main factors which influence the cooking times for rice are:
• the quantity of rice and size of container
• the quantity and heat of the water or other liquid
• the type of rice used
• the degree of heat created by the microwaves.

Cooking times can be guidelines only as the texture of cooked rice depends on personal preference, its use in or with other foods and its requirements for further cooking or reheating. For firmer or softer texture, use the shorter or middle cooking times, testing near the completion of the standing time; cook longer if required.

Always select a deep bowl or dish when cooking rice in the microwave oven, allowing plenty of space for boil-up but not boil-overs. Cover rice with double the quantity of boiling water. Cover *loosely* with a lid or

quality plastic film and take care when removing the cover, directing enclosed steam away to avoid burnt hands or face.

Cook at 100% power and stand for 5–10 minutes before serving. Stir rice occasionally during both the cooking and standing times with a fork so as to avoid mushing the grains whilst releasing excess or entrapped steam for a dry, more fluffy grain.

## PASTA
Packaged pasta may be cooked very easily in the microwave oven — an added advantage when preparing the whole dish by the same cooking method. Short pasta pieces are most suitable or you can break spaghetti into short lengths. The actual

cooking time is not a great deal less as, no matter what heating method is used, the dried pasta must first rehydrate in the hot water before it can be cooked. The savings in possible boil-overs are the added bonus.

Put pasta in a large deep bowl, cover with enough boiling water to immerse pasta completely and add 1 tablespoon oil. Cook at 100% power, stirring occasionally, until pasta is just tender. Stand 5 minutes before draining and serving.

Cooked pasta reheats to perfection in a microwave oven, producing still-firm separate pieces. Add a little oil and toss gently with a fork before reheating to avoid mashing the mixture.

## Vegetable Biryani

*Preparation time:*
  15 minutes
*Cooking time:*
  21 minutes
*Serves* 4

2 *tablespoons oil*
2 *teaspoons garam
  masala*
¼ *teaspoon turmeric*
1½ *cups long-grain
  white rice*
2 *cups hot vegetable or
  chicken stock*
2 *teaspoons curry paste*
2 *cardamom pods*
3 *cm piece cinnamon
  stick*
250 *g cauliflower, cut
  into florets*
250 *g green beans,
  trimmed and halved*
1 *tomato, sliced, for
  garnish*

1  Use 100% (High)
power throughout.
2  Pour oil into a 4-litre
casserole. Heat for
30–60 seconds. Add
garam masala, turmeric,
rice and stock. Cover
with lid or plastic wrap.
Cook for 10–12
minutes, stirring halfway
through cooking.
3  Blend curry paste with
5 tablespoons boiling
water. Stir into rice with
the cardamom and
cinnamon stick. Cover.
Cook for 1 minute.
4  Mix cauliflower and
beans into rice. Cover.
Cook for 5–7 minutes or
until cauliflower is
tender. Garnish with
tomato. Serve with
mango chutney.

## Tagliatelle with Spinach

*Preparation time:*
  10 minutes
*Cooking time:*
  20 minutes
*Serves* 1

125 *g frozen spinach*
3 *nests tagliatelle pasta*
2½ *cups boiling water*
60 *g cream cheese*
3 *tablespoons cream*
¼ *teaspoon nutmeg*
¼ *cup shredded
  Cheddar cheese*

1  Place spinach on a
microsafe plate. Cook
on 30% (Defrost) power
for 4–6 minutes.
Squeeze out water. Set
aside.
2  Place pasta in a 1-litre
casserole. Add water.
Cover with lid or plastic
wrap. Cook on 100%
(High) power for 6–8
minutes. Allow to stand,
covered, for 3 minutes.
3  Combine spinach,
cream cheese, cream and
nutmeg. Cook on 100%
(High) power for 2–3
minutes.
4  Drain pasta. Toss
with spinach mixture.
Sprinkle with cheese.
Serve with salad.

## Tuna Spirals

*Preparation time:*
  15 minutes
*Cooking time:*
  23 minutes
*Makes* 2

2 cups pasta spirals
3 cups boiling water
1 onion, finely chopped
1 cup chopped, canned
  tomatoes
1 cup tuna, drained
¼ teaspoon dried basil
¼ teaspoon dried
  oregano

1  Use 100% (High) power throughout.
2  Place pasta in a 1-litre casserole. Add water. Cover with lid or plastic wrap. Cook for 12–15 minutes. Allow to stand, covered, for 3 minutes.
3  Combine remaining ingredients in a small bowl. Cover with plastic wrap. Cook for 6–7 minutes, stirring halfway through cooking.
4  Drain pasta. Spoon onto serving plate. Top with tuna mixture. Sprinkle with Parmesan cheese, if desired. Serve with salad.

*Tuna Spira'*

# Smoked Fish and Rice

*Preparation time:*
  10 minutes
*Cooking time:*
  8 minutes
*Serves* 2

1 ¼ cups basmati rice
  (see Note)
1 ½ cups boiling water
2 small bay leaves
pinch ground turmeric
ground pepper
250 g smoked, boneless
  fish fillet, skinned
30 g butter
6–8 spring onions or
  shallots, sliced
2 tablespoons frozen
  peas
⅓ cup cream

1  Use 100% (High) power throughout.
2  Place rice in large, microsafe bowl; add boiling water, bay leaves, turmeric and seasonings to taste. Cover; cook for 5 minutes.
3  Stir rice well. Cut fillet in half; place on top of rice. Dot with the butter; sprinkle with onions and peas. Cover; cook until fish is tender, about 3 minutes.
4  Flake fish into large pieces with a fork. Add cream and stir through. Serve at once.

**Note:** Basmati rice cooks faster than regular long-grain rice because it is finer. If you use long-grain rice, rinse it thoroughly first in water. Proceed with Step 2, adding 5 minutes to cooking time.

> ## HINT
> When defrosting frozen fish, place them on a sheet of paper towel to absorb excess moisture. Do not allow to fully thaw before cooking as much of the natural fish juices will have seeped from the flesh, leaving it a little dry and tasteless.

> ## HINT
> To remove fishy odour from your microwave, heat 1 cup water in a large bowl with 4 or 5 slices of lemon (or 2 tablespoons vinegar) at 100% power for 3–4 minutes. Wipe out oven interior with a clean, dry cloth, and leave door open at least 5 minutes.

# Prawn and Cashew Pilau

*Preparation time:*
  15 minutes
*Cooking time:*
  12 minutes
*Serves* 1

185 g medium green
  king prawns
1 small onion, finely
  chopped
1 tablespoon vegetable
  or olive oil
¼ cup long-grain white
  rice
⅓ cup salted cashew
  nuts
¼ teaspoon turmeric
1 cup boiling water
fresh parsley or
  coriander to garnish

1  Use 100% (High) power throughout.
2  Peel and devein prawns; halve, if large.
3  In shallow, microsafe dish, combine onion and oil; cook until softened, 1 minute. Add rice and stir well. Cook 1 minute; add the cashew nuts.
4  Whisk turmeric into boiling water; pour into rice and mix well. Cover with plastic wrap; cook for 8 minutes. Stir in all prawns; cover and cook until rice is tender and liquid absorbed, 4 minutes more. Serve garnished with parsley.

*Prawn and Cashew Pilau, Smoked Fish and Rice*

# VEGETABLES AND FRUIT

*Vegetable Platter with Hazelnut Dressing (page 58)*

*The microwave oven is ideal for cooking vegetables. It offers shorter cooking times and the ability to cook with little or no water, resulting in true flavours and colours, excellent textures and improved nutrient retention.*

*Choose a microsafe cooking and serving container which will hold the vegetables snugly, with little or no space above them, as small quantities cooked in large containers will dry out on the top and edges. Broad, shallow containers cook more evenly than narrow, deep ones.*

*If the right container cannot be found, wrap bundles of vegetables in microsafe plastic wrap, oven bags or freezer bags, leaving a vent for steam, and then cook in any microsafe container.*

*A covered container will trap the steam during cooking for the best tender-crisp results, but the wrong cover can result in uneven cooking, and tough or dehydrated textures.*

*Choose your cover from the following:*
● *microsafe plastic wrap for use over containers (slashed for venting), or for bundle-wrapping;*
● *microsafe plastic oven or freezer bags (without metal ties); or*
● *microsafe lid of the cooking container.*

## PREPARATION AND ARRANGEMENT
● Cut vegetables into uniform pieces or portions; they'll cook most evenly.
● Allow for different sizes and densities when cooking mixed vegetables. Large, firm vegetables or those low in moisture take longer to cook, so place these around the outside of the container. Place small or high-moisture vegetables which require shorter cooking times in the centre. Alternatively, start cooking large, firm, low-moisture vegetables first, then add the small, high-moisture vegetables in delayed sequences so that all finish cooking at the same time.
● Position unevenly-shaped vegetables (broccoli or cauliflower, asparagus spears or root vegetables) in container so the thickest parts are at the outer edges.
● Small vegetables (peas) or cut pieces (diced carrots) should be stirred once or twice during cooking, especially when in a small, deep container.

● Large vegetables or pieces should be turned or repositioned.

## COOKING TECHNIQUES
Vegetables vary in textures, shapes and sizes, so choose the most appropriate of the three basic microwaving methods to achieve the most suitable results:
1 Cook with no water (or just the moisture clinging after washing) and with a cover.
2 Cook with 1–2 tablespoons water, and with a cover.
3 For potatoes and other vegetables which have their own protective skin, cook with no water OR cover.

*Avoid adding salt to cooking water.* It draws moisture from vegetables and can even toughen them. You'll find microwaving intensifies natural flavours anyway, so taste and add salt, if you must, *after cooking.*

All vegetables, especially green ones, offer the best quality and nutrition when completely cooked by microwave and served immediately, without standing time. The exceptions are potatoes and pumpkin. The final texture is improved if these dense vegetables are cooked almost through, then left to stand, covered, to finish cooking with residual heat.

A good rule to follow when cooking several courses for a meal by microwave is to *cook the vegetables last*, while the main dish or dessert stands.

## Stewing

For High-Moisture Fruits (apples, berries, rhubarb):
- Slice or chop as desired; add spices (and sugar, if using).
- Use a microsafe container just large enough to hold the fruit.
- *Add little or no water.*
- Closely cover with container lid, or use microsafe plastic wrap only slightly vented.
- Sample cooking time: 500 g of sliced apples with 2 tablespoons each of sugar and water will cook in 5–6 minutes. Use more or less time, depending on texture desired.

For Low-Moisture Fruits (bananas, pears, dried fruits):
- Use more liquid or syrup as needed to rehydrate, but use a larger container to avoid boil-overs.
- Before adding large dried fruits to mixtures, be sure to chop and soak until soft.

## Poaching
- Peel, halve, core or stone the fruit (leave small stone fruits whole, if desired); place in deep, microsafe dish.
- Cover fruit with a liquid: fruit juice, white or red wine, fortified wine (or mixture of any of these and water), or a sugar syrup.
- Add spices: whole allspice, cloves or cinnamon sticks. Ground spices can be used, but they will 'tarnish' an otherwise clear syrup.
- Cover and cook until tender when pierced with a fine skewer, 5–8 minutes (turn any whole stone fruit which float after 3 minutes).

## Baking

Apples: Core 4 apples; cut a thin slice off bases so that they stand upright. Slit around 'equator' of each to avoid splitting. Stuff cores with mixture of dried fruit, butter, brown sugar and spices.

Place in round dish deep enough to prevent plastic cover touching the filling; do not vent. (Add a little water or fruit juice, extra sugar and butter if extra syrup is desired.) Cook 8–10 minutes.

Bananas: In microsafe dish, heat lemon juice, brown sugar, butter and spices until sugar melts. Stir in sliced bananas; cook until heated, but not soft.

Grapefruit: Halve crosswise and separate into segments with grapefruit knife. Sprinkle to taste with brown sugar and sherry. Add 1 teaspoon butter. Cook, uncovered, until warm, about 1 minute.

## Jams and Jellies
- Cook small quantities at a time (2 cups strawberries, 1 kg stone fruits or, for marmalade, 4 or 5 oranges or lemons).
- Use a large, wide microsafe bowl for quick evaporation and to prevent boil-overs.
- Test for setting in the usual way; bottle in sterilised jars. Cool, then seal.

• If using paraffin wax for sealing, heat conventionally, as it will not melt successfully by microwave.

> **HINT**
> Never place an unopened or opened can in a microwave oven. Always pour contents into a recommended microsafe container and cook as directed.

## FROZEN, CANNED OR DRIED VEGETABLES

With home frozen or commercially frozen vegetables, take out the amount required; reseal packet and return to freezer at once. Microwave the portion in a suitable container as packet directs.

To cook the whole packet, slash a few vents in packet for steam. Cook in a suitable container or directly on oven shelf or turntable (line container or shelf first with plastic wrap or paper towels to prevent any packaging dyes from staining it).

When using canned vegetables, drain contents of can, reserving 1 or 2 tablespoons of the liquid. Place vegetables in a suitable container; add reserved liquid and cover. Microwave at 100% (High) power until just heated through, 1–2 minutes.

Reconstitute dehydrated and dried vegetables by soaking in water as packet directs; drain, if recipe directs, and reheat.

## FRUIT

Fruit cooked by microwave retains a wonderful, fresh-picked flavour and colour that no other cooking method can match. Another reward is the quickness of the procedure. For maximum nutrition, cook fruit with skin attached, particularly when serving invalids. *Reduce sugar*. Some fruits which need sweetening when cooked conventionally do not need it when microwaved.

Cook at 100% (High) power generally, unless otherwise recommended but, to retain the shape of fruit when needed, reduce to 50–30% (Medium to Low). Precise cooking times are impossible to gauge; fruit varieties and seasonal changes have their effects. Refer to oven manual or cookbooks for instructions for individual fruits.

Do not allow plastic wrap covers to touch fruit mixtures with a butter or sugar content during cooking. The high heat generated can melt them.

Frozen fruit should not be completely defrosted by microwave. It should be still cold, firm and slightly icy for best flavour and texture. To speed thawing, break fruit up with a fork or, if in plastic pouches, gently flex pouch occasionally to distribute fruit and juices.

> **HINT**
> Always tip canned fruit or vegetables into a microsafe dish, together with their juice or liquid, as this contains valuable water-soluble vitamins and other nutrients.

# Vegetable Platter with Hazelnut Dressing

*Preparation time:*
   20 minutes
*Cooking time:*
   14 minutes
*Serves* 6

*50 g hazelnuts*
*1 small cauliflower, cut into even-sized florets*
*200 g green beans*
*200 g broccoli, cut into even-sized florets*
*2 tablespoons water*
*1 red capsicum, cut into strips*
*1 x 225 g can baby corn, drained*
*3 carrots, cut into strips*
*60 g butter*
*2 tablespoons oil*
*2 teaspoons white wine vinegar*

1  Use 100% (High) power throughout.
2  Place hazelnuts on a microsafe dinner plate. Cook for 2–3 minutes, stirring halfway through cooking.
3  Using a tea-towel, rub the skin off the nuts. Return any nuts that do not peel easily for a further 30–60 seconds. Finely chop nuts. Set aside.
4  Arrange cauliflower, beans and broccoli in separate piles on a large, shallow, microsafe serving dish. Add water. Cover with plastic wrap. Cook for 4–5 minutes.
5  Add capsicum, corn and carrots in separate piles to dish. Re-cover. Cook for a further 4–6 minutes.
6  Put butter and oil in a small bowl. Cook for 1½–2 minutes. Add nuts, vinegar and pepper. Mix well. Cook for a further 30–60 seconds.
7  Drain any water from the vegetables. Pour over the hot dressing.

### HINT
To peel tomatoes, peaches, etc., lightly slash or prick the skin of the fruit, place on a microsafe plate and heat on 100% (High) power for 30–40 seconds per piece. Timing varies with ripeness, size and firmness. Remove skin with a small knife.

## FRESH VEGETABLE

| VEGETABLE | AMOUNT |
|---|---|
| Asparagus | 500 g |
| Beans | 500 g |
| Broccoli | 500 g |
| Brussels sprouts | 500 g |
| Cabbage | 500 g |
| Carrots | 500 g |
| Cauliflower | 500 g |
| | 500 g |
| Corn (on cob) | 500 g (2) |
| | 1 kg (4) |
| Mushrooms | 500 g |
| Peas (green) | 500 g |
| (snow) | 500 g |
| Potatoes (jacket) | 2 medium |
| | 4 small |
| (baked) | 2 medium |
| | 4 small |
| Pumpkin | 500 g |
| Spinach | 500 g |
| Squash | 500 g |
| Sweet Potato | 2 whole |
| | 4 whole |
| Tomatoes | 500 g |
| Zucchini | 500 g |

# COOKING CHART

| COOKING PROCEDURE | MICROWAVE TIME AT 100% (HIGH) |
|---|---|
| Wash and place in a freezer bag | 3–4 minutes |
| Cut into 4 cm pieces. Cook in 1-litre casserole with 1 tablespoon water. Cover. | 4–5 minutes |
| Cut into uniform florets. Arrange with flower towards centre. Cover. | 3–4 minutes |
| Arrange in a 23-cm flan dish. Arrange with stalk towards outside. Cover. | 3–4 minutes |
| Shred and cook in a 1.5-litre casserole with 2 tablespoons water. Cover. | 4–5 minutes |
| Arrange in a 1-litre casserole. Combine carrots with 1 tablespoon water. Cover. | 4–5 minutes |
| WHOLE: wash well. Place on a dinner plate. Cover with plastic wrap; turn over after 3 minutes. Stand covered with foil for 5 minutes. | 10–12 minutes |
| Cut into uniform florets. Arrange with flower towards centre, with 1 tablespoon water. Cover. | 4–5 minutes |
| Arrange in a 1-litre casserole with ¼ cup water. Cover. Turn over during cooking | 7–9 minutes |
| Arrange in a 1.5-litre casserole with ⅓ cup water. Cover. Turn over during cooking. | 15–17 minutes |
| Sliced or whole. Place in a 1-litre casserole with 2 teaspoons butter. Cover. | 2–3 minutes |
| Cook in a 1-litre casserole with 1 teaspoon sugar and 1 tablespoon water. Cover. | 2–4 minutes |
| Remove string from pod. Cook in a 1-litre casserole with 1 tablespoon water. | 3–4 minutes |
| Pierce skin with a fork. Place on turntable. Turn over halfway through cooking. Allow to stand wrapped in foil. | 4–5 minutes |
| Peel and quarter potatoes. Cook, covered, in a 1-litre casserole dish with ½ cup water. | 5–6 minutes |
| Peel and cut into serving-size pieces. Place in a 1-litre casserole. Cover. | 4–6 minutes |
| Wash and shred. Cook, covered, in a 1.5-litre casserole with 2 tablespoons water. | 4–6 minutes |
| Wash and place in a casserole with 1 tablespoon of butter or water. Cover. Pierce whole squash with a fork. | 4–5 minutes |
| Peel and quarter potatoes. Cook, covered, in a 1-litre casserole with ½ cup water. | 4–5 minutes |
| Cut into quarters. Place in a 1-litre casserole. Season and cover. | 2–3 minutes |
| Cut into uniform-size pieces. Place in a 1-litre casserole with 1 tablespoon water and 1 tablespoon butter. Cover. | 5–6 minutes |

**HINT**
Pierce whole unpeeled vegetables, such as squash, potatoes, baby pumpkin and tomatoes.

**HINT**
After microwaving vegetables, add butter, margarine, yoghurt, lemon juice, herbs and spices — or a sauce, as desired.

# Blackberry and Apple Pudding

*Preparation time:*
  25 minutes
*Cooking time:*
  10 minutes + 10
  minutes standing
*Serves* 4

750 g *Granny Smith*
  *apples*
2 tablespoons lemon
  *juice*
375 g *fresh or frozen*
  *blackberries*
3 tablespoons icing
  *sugar*
125 g *butter at room*
  *temperature*
½ cup *caster sugar*
1 cup *self-raising flour,*
  *sifted*
1 teaspoon baking
  *powder*
2 *eggs*

1  Use 100% (High) power throughout.
2  Quarter and core apples. Cut a few thin slices. Coat with a little of the lemon juice to prevent browning. Reserve for decoration. Peel and chop remaining apple. Toss in lemon juice.
3  Place half the apple in a microsafe bowl. Set aside remaining apples. Reserve a few blackberries for decoration. Add remainder to bowl. Cover with plastic wrap. Cook for 6–8 minutes, stirring halfway through cooking.
4  Place fruit in a food processor or blender. Process until smooth. Rub through a fine sieve to remove pips. Stir in icing sugar. Set aside.
5  Place butter, sugar, flour, baking powder and eggs in a bowl. Beat for 2 minutes or until smooth. Stir in reserved chopped apple. Spoon mixture into a greased, 1-litre microsafe dish. Smooth top.
6  Cover dish loosely with plastic wrap. Cook for 6–8 minutes. Stand

for 10 minutes.
7 Reheat fruit sauce for 1–2 minutes. Unmould pudding onto serving plate. Pour a little sauce over pudding. Decorate with reserved fruit. Serve remaining sauce separately.

# Caramel Pears

*Preparation time:*
 10 minutes
*Cooking time:*
 4 minutes
*Serves 4*

60 g butter
½ cup brown sugar
½ cup cream
2 teaspoons brandy
4 pears, slightly soft, peeled
ground cinnamon (optional)

1 Melt butter in a microsafe jug on 70% (Medium High) power for 1 minute. Stir in sugar. Cook a further 2 minutes.
2 Blend in cream and brandy. Cook on 100% (High) power for 30 seconds.
3 Place pears on a serving platter, cover and cook on 100% (High) power for 1 minute or until just tender. Pour over sauce. Sprinkle with a little cinnamon before serving, if liked.

---

HINT
To soften solidly frozen ice-cream: microwave a 2-litre container at 30% power for 20–40 seconds. Stand, then repeat the process as needed.

*Blackberry and Apple Pudding, Caramel Pears*

# Strawberry Jam

*Preparation time:*
  10 minutes
*Cooking time:*
  25 minutes + 5
  minutes standing
*Makes* 2 cups

2 x 250 g punnets
  *strawberries*
¼ *cup lemon juice*
2 *cups sugar*

1  Use 100% (High)
power throughout.

2  Wash and hull strawberries. Chop roughly. Place in a large microsafe bowl or jug with lemon juice. Cook, covered, for 3–4 minutes or until soft.

3  Stir in sugar until dissolved. Cook, uncovered, for about 20 minutes, stirring occasionally until jam sets when tested (see Note). Stand for 5 minutes.

4  Pour into warm sterilised jars. Seal. Store jars in refrigerator.

**Note**: To test for setting: put a spoonful of jam on a chilled saucer. Leave to stand for 3 minutes. Run a fingertip through jam. If it wrinkles and fingertip leaves a trail, it is ready.

*Strawberry Jam*

# INDEX

Accessories 7
Aluminium
  egg rings 9
  foil *see* Foil
  skewers 9
Apples
  baking 56
  and Blackberry Pudding
    60, *61*
Arranging food 13–14

Baking
  custard 44
  fruit 56
Baking paper 7
Bamboo skewers 9
Bananas, baking 56
Basketware 11
Beef
  roasting 22
  and Vegetables, Chinese
    24, *24*
Blackberry and Apple
  Pudding 60, *61*
Boiling eggs 43
Bowls 7
Bread 19
Browning aids 23
Browning dishes 8, 11
Browning foods 15
Butter, to melt 45

Cans 57
  seafood 38
  vegetables 57
Caramel Pears 61, *61*
Care of your oven 5
Casseroling
  meat 21–22
  poultry 30
Cheese 43
Chicken
  fat-free cooking 30–31
  self-basting 31
  Breasts in Almond Sauce
    34, *35*
  Soy and Honey 28, 32

Tandoori, with
  Cucumber Salad 28, 31
Chicken Liver Pâté 34, *34*
Chilli con Carne 27, *27*
China 11
Chinese Beef and
  Vegetables 24, *24*
Clarified Butter 45
Cleaning your oven 5
Cod Pockets 40, *41*
Composition of food 13
Containers 6–7
Cooking pouches 11
Cooking techniques 12–15
Cookware 6, 6–11
Covering food 8–9, 15
Crisper-griddles 11
Crumbed seafood 38
Custard
  baked 44
  sauces 43

Dairy foods 42–47
Defrosting 16–17
  fish 38, 52
  fruit and vegetables 57
Density of food 13
Dried fruits 56
Dried vegetables 57
Duck, fat-free cooking 31

Earthenware 11
Egg rings 9
Eggs 42–47
  Florentine 42, *45*
  Spanish Omelette *42*, 44
Elevated racks 9

Fat-free cooking of
  poultry 30–31
Fat from meat 23
Fish 36–41
  defrosting 38, 52
  fillets 37
  whole 37
Foam trays 19
Foil 9, 11, 17, 18,
  shielding with 23, 29
Freezer bags 8, 11
Freezing 18–19
Frozen food *see* Defrosting
Fruit 54–62
  Roly-Poly with Orange
    Cream 47, *47*
Frying 45

Ghee 45
Glass 11
Glaze 29
Grapefruit, baking 56
Greaseproof paper 7

Herbs 23

Ice-cream, to soften 61
Installing your oven 4

Jam 56–57
  Strawberry 62, *62*
Jellies 56–57
Jugs 7

Lamb
  roasting 22
  Rack of 26, *26*
  Rosemary *20*, 23

Maintenance 5
Marinades 23
Meat 20–27
  defrosting 19
  roasting 22
Metal 11
  *see also* Aluminium
  pans 7
Microwave oven described
  3
Microwaves
  defined 3
  how they cook 3–4
Milk 43
  sauces 44
Mince 27
  Chilli con Carne 27, *27*
Mussels
  to open 38
  Creamy Baked 40, *41*

Odour, to remove 52
Omelette, Spanish *42*, 44
Oven bags 8, 11
  meat 22–23
  poultry 30
Oysters
  to open 38
  Kilpatrick 39, *39*

Paper 7, 11
Pasta 48–53
  Spirals with Tuna 50, *51*
  Tagliatelle with Spinach
    *48*, 50

Pâté, Chicken Liver 34, *34*
Pears, Caramel 61, *61*
Peeling tomatoes, peaches etc. *58*
Piercing foods 14
Pilau, Prawn and Cashew 52, *53*
Pizzas 18
Plastic 11
    wrap 8, 11
Poaching
    eggs 43–44
    fruit 56
Pork
    roasting 22
    Sesame 25, *25*
Pot roasting 21
Pottery 11
Poultry 29–35
    defrosting 19
    pieces 30
    whole birds 29
Power levels 4, 5
Prawn and Cashew Pilau 52, *53*
Probes 9
Pudding
    Apple and Blackberry 60, *61*
    Queen 46, *47*

Quantity of food 12
Queen of Puddings 46, *47*

Rack of Lamb 26, *26*
Racks 9, 13
    poultry 32
Radiation 4–5

Reheating 14
    fish 38
    poultry 31
Rice 48–53
    Prawn and Cashew Pilau 52, *53*
    and Smoked Fish 52, *53*
    Vegetable Biryani 48, *50*
Roasting
    meat 21, 22
    poultry 29
Roasting racks 9
Roasts, defrosting 18
Roly-Poly, Fruit, with Orange Cream 47, *47*
Rosemary Lamb 20, *23*

Safety 4–5
Salmon, with Lime Mayonnaise 36, *38*
Salt
    meat 23
    vegetables 55
Salted fish 38
Sauces 18
Scrambling eggs 44
Self-basting poultry 31
Sesame Pork 25, *25*
Shape of food 12
Shellfish 36–41
Shielding with foil 17, 23, 29
Shortcuts 10, 17
Size of food 12
Skewers 9
Slashing foods 14
Smoked fish 38
    and Rice 52, *53*

Soy and Honey Chicken 28, *32*
Spanish Omelette *42*, 44
Spices 56
Spinach with Tagliatelle 48, *50*
Standing time 10, 14
Starting temperature 13
Stewing fruit 56
Strawberry Jam 62, *62*
Stuffing poultry 29

Tagliatelle with Spinach 48, *50*
Tandoori Chicken with Cucumber Salad 28, *31*
Techniques 12–15
Temperature, starting 13
Thawing *see* Defrosting
Thermometers 9, 21
Timing foods 14
Tomatoes, to peel 58
Trussing poultry 32
Tuna Spirals 50, *51*
Turkey 31
    self-basting 31
    Slices with Orange Cream Sauce 32, *33*

Veal, roasting 22
Vegetables 54–62
    Biryani 48, *50*
    Platter with Hazelnut Dressing 54, *58*

White sauce 44
Wood 11

## GLOSSARY

| | | |
|---|---|---|
| burghul | = | cracked wheat |
| capsicum | = | sweet pepper |
| cornflour | = | cornstarch |
| eggplant | = | aubergine |
| pepitas | = | dried, untoasted pumpkin seeds |
| shallots | = | spring onions |
| snow pea | = | mangetout |
| zucchini | = | courgettes |